HOW TO
SAVE THE
WHOLE
BLINKIN'
PLANET

ALSO BY LEE CONSTABLE

How to Save the Whole Stinkin' Planet

HOW TO SAVE THE WHOLE BLINKIN' PLANET

A RENEWABLE ENERGY ADVENTURE!

LEE CONSTABLE

Illustrated by **AŚKA**

PUFFIN BOOKS

PUFFIN BOOKS

UK | USA | Canada | Ireland | Australia
India | New Zealand | South Africa | China

Penguin Random House Australia is part of the Penguin Random House group of companies whose addresses can be found at global.penguinrandomhouse.com.

First published by Puffin Books, an imprint of Penguin Random House Australia, in 2024

Cover and internal illustrations by Aśka
Design by Caroline Lee © Penguin Random House Australia Pty Ltd

Printed and bound in Australia by Griffin Press, an accredited ISO AS/NZS 14001 Environmental Management Systems printer

 A catalogue record for this book is available from the National Library of Australia

ISBN 978 1 76134 082 6

penguin.com.au

MIX
Paper | Supporting
responsible forestry
FSC® C018684

We at Penguin Random House Australia acknowledge that Aboriginal and Torres Strait Islander peoples are the Traditional Custodians and the first storytellers of the lands on which we live and work. We honour Aboriginal and Torres Strait Islander peoples' continuous connection to Country, waters, skies and communities. We celebrate Aboriginal and Torres Strait Islander stories, traditions and living cultures; and we pay our respects to Elders past and present.

To everyday heroes of all ages trying to make
the blinkin' planet a better place.

∧∧∧ CONTENTS ∧∧∧

So . . . you want to be a superhero? AND save the whole blinkin' planet too? Well, you've picked up the right book!

Our planet is full of everyday heroes making it a better place. Do you have a hero? Who are they? And why are they a hero to you?

You seem very keen, bright and ready for anything. But, before we dive into action, we should talk about what the blink this planet even needs to be saved from.

Here are some different ways heroes save the whole blinkin' planet every day:
*   protecting plants and animals from extinction
*   saving water
*   reducing, reusing, recycling and repairing things
*   being kind to people and taking care of each other.

What's a way that YOU like to help make the world a better place? Do you have a superpower up your sleeve that helps you do that?

Electricity – an everyday SUPERPOWER

One of our everyday superpowers is ELECTRICITY. Electricity is a type of ENERGY that humans have been experimenting with for hundreds of years. Without electricity we wouldn't have any of the electronic devices that make our lives better – from fridges to lights and computers to smartphones. But even things that *aren't* directly powered by electricity – like this book – are often made by factories and processes that use electricity. And transported to bookstores and to you in vehicles that use energy through fuel such as petrol, diesel or maybe even electricity.

Yep – this very book was made using electricity and other types of energy, and I bet electricity and fuel for transport had something to do with creating the clothes you're wearing, your shoes, your toys, your pens and pencils, your sports gear, your hats and hair ties, and your favourite games – *GASP!* Sorry, I start listing things sometimes and forget to breathe! The point is our lives are energised and powered and fuelled in so many ways that we may not even realise until we really put our thinking hard hats on.

What's the big blinkin' problem?

How we POWER our everyday lives is putting the planet under a lot of stress and things are heating up! Many of the ways we electrify and fuel our lives lead to POLLUTION called GREENHOUSE GASES that cause changes in our weather systems and global temperature and more. This is called global warming or CLIMATE CHANGE. We can't keep this up, so things have to change fast. That's why we need bright sparks like you. With all this brainpower we can save the whole blinkin' planet! Together!

What am I meant to do about that?

Not 'I'! Not 'you'! WE! What are WE meant to do about this? That's the question. You won't be taking on this challenge alone. On this mission you will investigate the types of energy we are using to make the electricity and fuel that powers our lives. Feel free to invite your friends, family and other favourite humans along for the ride too. The more, the hairier! I mean, scarier! Or was it the more the 'merrier'? I forget.

The point is, we're a force to be reckoned with. We need to figure out together how we can reduce the impact our energy use has on the whole blinkin' planet.

Join the ELECTRIFYING adventure! If we're successful in our mission, we will have a blueprint to save the blinkin' planet and YOU will graduate from Imagineering Academy. I understand that's your lifelong dream. If it isn't, then it blinkin' well will be by the end.

IMAGINEERING
101

At this point you might be thinking, 'What the blinkin' heck is an <u>IMAGINEER?</u>'

I'm glad you asked. Asking questions is one of the most important skills you'll need for the mission ahead.

Imagineer is a combination of two different words: **imagination** and **engineer**.

Professional engineers have had a lot of training to do what they do, but every engineer (or imagineer for that matter) starts somewhere. It's okay if you're brand-new to this! You might discover you've been doing some DIY imagineering already.

So, what do you think an imagineer might do? What types of skills do you think they have? And what big blinkin' problems might they solve?

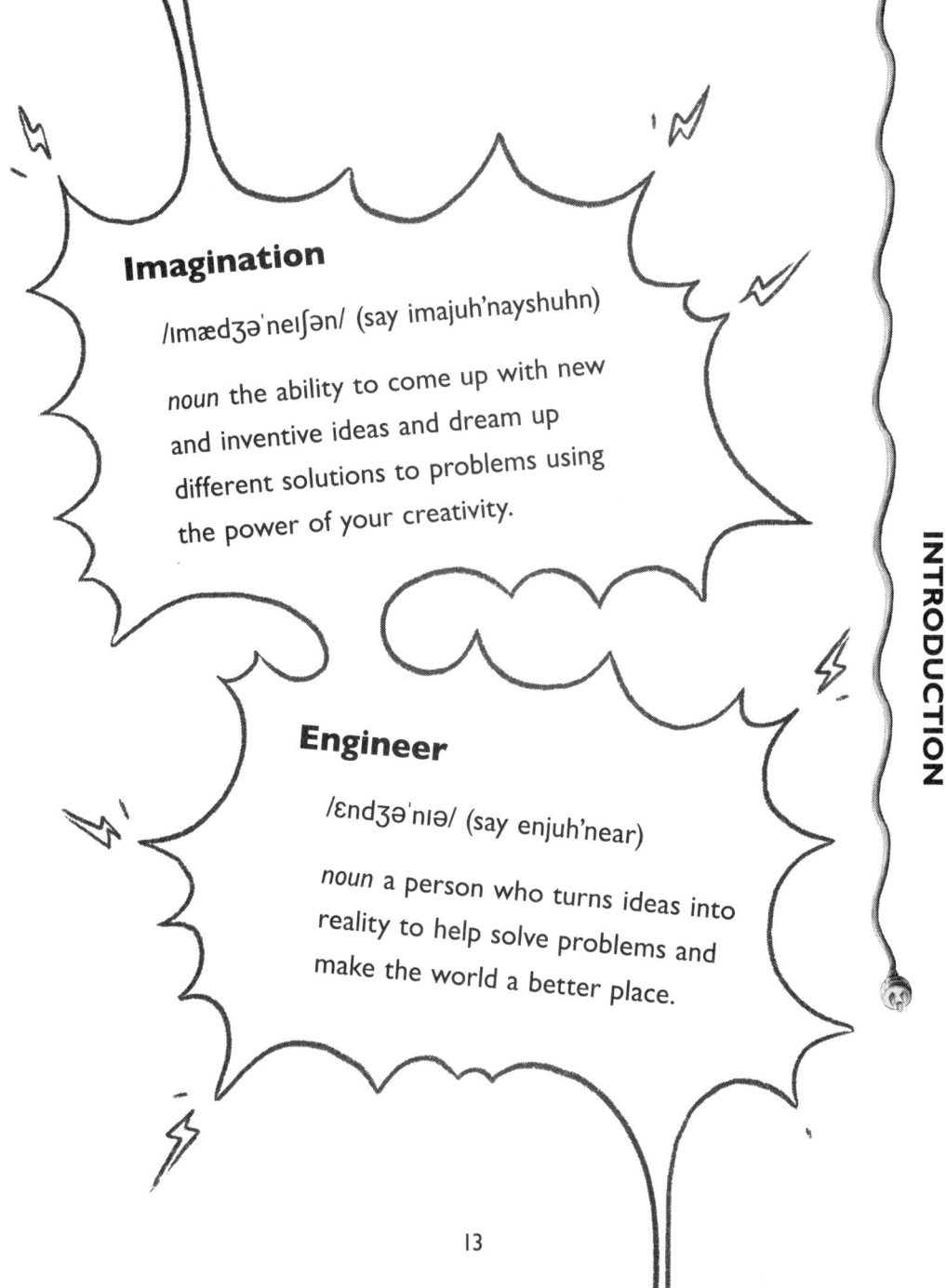

Imagination

/ɪmædʒəˈneɪʃən/ (say imajuh'nayshuhn)

noun the ability to come up with new and inventive ideas and dream up different solutions to problems using the power of your creativity.

Engineer

/ɛndʒəˈnɪə/ (say enjuh'near)

noun a person who turns ideas into reality to help solve problems and make the world a better place.

Imagineers are engineers who like to use our powers of imagination, creativity and problem-solving to come up with wild and wonderful ideas and inventions that make the whole blinkin' world run as smoothly and safely as possible. Our planet needs all the brainpower it can get, so please accept the mission to join the adventure of a lifetime.

Do you think you're up for it? If so, let the journey begin.

AN IMPORTANT NOTE ON ELECTRICAL SAFETY

Electricity is invisible but it is very dangerous and should never be touched, otherwise you will receive an electrical shock that could kill you! Don't ever touch power points and make sure an adult supervises you plugging in electrical devices and cords. Always check with an adult before touching any electrical devices.

HOW TO USE THIS BOOK

I'm breaking each stage of this journey down into parts. This will help us navigate through our quest.

SWITCH ON

These quick questions are to warm up your brain for the challenges ahead and get you ready for the skills you're about to master and the know-how you'll gain.

SNAPSHOT

This is a chance to get a picture of what things are like right now and get our heads around some of the big blinkin' problems we need to tackle.

BLINK FORWARD

This is where our imagineering skills (and my superpower) come into play. We'll put our heads together, close our eyes and flash ourselves forward into the bright future we want to create.

GET ACTIVE

Whenever you see this lightning bolt, that's a sign that it's time to turn our thinking into doing. Scan the QR code displayed on the electro-thinga-bob-a-doo-hicky to complete a virtual quiz online.

LIGHTNING QUIZ

This is your chance to level up using the new knowledge and skills you've gained. Put yourself to the test to advance to the next stage of Imagineering Academy and get one giant leap closer to saving the whole blinkin' planet!

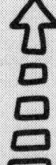

LEVEL UP

Huzzah! This is a chance to pat ourselves on the back for our achievements so far before we dive into the next adventure.

FLASH FACTS

You'll see these bits of interesting info peppered throughout this book. These will give you some powerful points to take with you and share with others too.

HAVE YOU HEARD THE WORD?

Greenhouse gases? Imagineering? Climate change? It can be hard to keep track of all the new words and phrases we're using on this adventure but worry not! I've imagineered a solution.

At the back of this training manual, you'll find a list of words and their meanings. So, if you ever see something that looks like THIS, you'll know you can flip to the Glossary at the back of the book and find out what it means in a flash!

FOR THIS ELECTRIFYING ADVENTURE YOU'LL NEED:

- A thinking hat – I recommend a hard hat like mine (real or imaginary)

- A tool belt full of handy gadgets, doo-hickies and thingamies

- An imagineer's notebook to jot down your ideas and discoveries, and draw your inventions

- A tonne of curiosity

- A heap of imagination

- An emergency snack

- All of your energy!

Got everything?

Good. Away we go!

CHAPTER ONE

WELCOME
TO
IMAGINEERING
ACADEMY

Allow me to introduce myself. My name is Captain Kilowatt. I'm an <u>ELECTRICAL ENGINEER</u> and an imagineering superhero – yes, you can be both. That's me in the tool belt, hard hat and the welding goggles. Gidday!

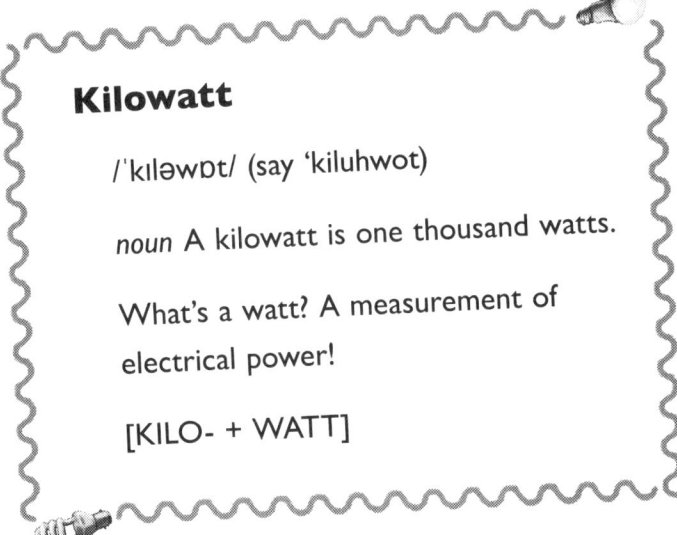

Kilowatt

/ˈkɪləwɒt/ (say ˈkiluhwot)

noun A kilowatt is one thousand watts.

What's a watt? A measurement of electrical power!

[KILO- + WATT]

Maybe you should put some eyewear on too because the future is looking BRIGHT! Well, it is now that *YOU'RE* here.

Did you eat your breakfast this morning? I sure hope so. Energy is super important. I get mine from a big bowl of cereal or some toast before I head out for a new day of adventure. And I've always got an emergency snack in my tool belt to keep me fuelled up and ready for action. You'll need that brain and body of yours to be energised and ready for anything if you're going to keep up with me!

Energy isn't just about what snacks you've got in your lunchbox (or your tool belt for that matter). Energy comes in many forms and from many sources – from the electricity that lights our homes, BATTERIES that power our devices, and the fuel that makes cars and planes go. Unfortunately, some of the ways we've been generating energy have caused problems for our planet – which causes even bigger blinkin' problems for us. Luckily there are things we can do to combat this. We'll get into all that soon!

First, let me bring you up to speed on the mission at hand then we can dive right in.

MISSION SPARKOLOGY

Our mission is to investigate how the world is powered and imagineer a brighter future in the blink of an eye!

TOOL-BELT TOUR

I see you've been admiring my imagineering outfit.

Do you know anyone who wears a hard hat like mine to work? What's their job?

Whatever it is, it must be something where they have to protect their big ol' brain. That's important. Safety first!

One of my favourite things about being an electrical engineer eco-superhero imagineer extraordinaire is getting to wear this awesome tool belt! Why? Because of all the sweet stuff I can carry with me — hands-free — on my adventures.

I'll take you on a tool-belt tour. Let's see . . . What have I got in here?

★ A drink bottle – hydration is important!

★ Tools for every occasion like a hammer, a spanner, pliers, and a screwdriver – with detachable, switchable heads . . .

★ An emergency banana

★ Some raisins, a muesli bar, a sandwich . . . Okay, there are A LOT of snacks in here. Gotta keep my energy up!

* A notebook to write down ideas.
* A multimeter – that's a device for measuring the flow of electricity.
* Some insulated safety gloves, a high-vis vest, a sign that says 'ELECTRIC SHOCK RISK! DO NOT TOUCH!' and some goggles for extra safety in a flash.

* And . . . I've saved my FAVOURITE thing for last . . . BEHOLD! MY **ELECTRO-THINGA-BOB-A-DOO-HICKY**!

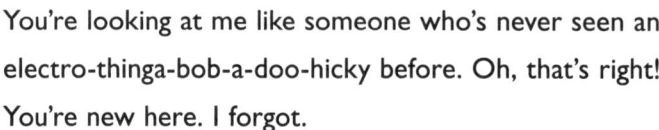

You're looking at me like someone who's never seen an electro-thinga-bob-a-doo-hicky before. Oh, that's right! You're new here. I forgot.

This device is something you only get from being an electrical engineer eco-superhero imagineer like me. You're already in Imagineering Academy so that brings you one step closer to getting one when you're an adult some day. Don't worry, though – you can watch me use mine on our adventures together!

What do you mean, 'What for?'

Oh! Right . . . new imagineer. Of course. You just seem so switched on. It's hard to believe this is your first day. Keep asking questions. That's a smart move.

The electro-thinga-bob-a-doo-hicky can be used for:

★ Anything and everything that any other hand-held electronic device can do

★ Zooming IN so we can see the tiniest of tiny details

★ Zooming waaay OUT so we can see the BIG blinkin' picture

★ Zapping us from A to B! Or from A to A-and-a-half if it's on the blink . . .

★ Displaying QR codes that you can scan to go to interactive online quizzes

★ Other things . . . probably! My electro-thinga-bob-a-doo-hicky is always surprising me, and an electrical engineer eco-superhero imagineer like me can always learn new tricks.

You might have noticed my tool belt can carry more than most. That's just another perk of my line of work!

THE INNOVATION CYCLE

INNOVATION

Today's news

Tomorrow's normal

ADOPTION

Imagineers (and other kinds of inventors and engineers too) use a process called the INNOVATION CYCLE to come up with, test out and improve their creations and ideas. It's super important to be open to making the solutions you think up even better and to change them up whenever new challenges or information comes your way.

It goes like this . . .

THINK

Use that brainpower of yours to noodle on the problem at hand. What needs fixing? Is that really the main problem or is there another problem causing that problem? Are there any other challenges you need to keep in mind? Once you know what the problem is you can come up with ideas for solutions. Writing down all your brainstormed ideas in your notebook will help. Don't second-guess. Just write. Think big! Think bold! Think BRIGHT! You can always rethink and refocus after your first big brainstorm.

DESIGN

Choose one idea from your brainstorm and draw it out on paper. Zoom in on the details of your imagined solution. What is it made of? What is its shape and size? How does it work? Does it move? Remember, your first design doesn't have to be perfect! Redesigning will almost certainly happen further down the road.

MAKE

Once you're happy with your first design, build it! It's okay if it's not perfect. This is called a PROTOTYPE. It's a 3D first draft of your innovative invention.

TEST

GIVE IT A WHIRL! See if your new creation works.

Did it solve the problem? Why? Or why not? What did you learn by putting it to the test? Is there anything you'd do differently? Go back to the thinking, designing and making steps to see if there are other questions you need to answer. Let those learnings sink in and try new things along the way. Don't forget to write things down. If you're like me then you tend to forget in all the excitement.

The cycle can keep going around as you keep improving on your idea. You can use what you learn from your test to rethink, redesign or remake your invention until you are happy with how it works.

And it's okay to try lots of different ideas too. Don't be afraid to go back to the drawing board and spend more time brainstorming and designing. There's no such thing as failure in this process. It's all about learning and experimenting. Your creation didn't do what you wanted it to? Great! That's an opportunity to learn something.

NEVER FEAR, SCIENCE IS HERE!

That's right, bright sparks. Not only am I, Captain Kilowatt, here with you on this journey but I've brought a whole tool belt full of fun and my secret superpower – science! Science allows us to learn about things by experimenting and observing.

In our Imagineering Academy training, we are going to be looking at not just these big blinkin' problems but the exciting solutions out there.

We're in this together. Two brains are better than one, so we'll put our heads together to imagineer the future we want to see. The more brains (and sets of hands) the better, so you can invite your friends, family, teachers and other people in your life to join us too.

Turn the page if you accept Mission Sparkology!

SPARKOLOGY RECRUIT CODENAME

Well done! Before we charge into things, you'll need an imagineer's codename and ID.

Find the first part of your codename next to the first letter of your name below:

A – The Glorious	**J – The Courageous**
B – The Legendary	**K – The Powerful**
C – The Extraordinary	**L – The Wise**
D – The Unbelievable	**M – The Brave**
E – The Brainy	**N – The Brilliant**
F – The Imaginative	**O – The Energetic**
G – The Curious	**P – The Great**
H – The Outrageous	**Q – The Honourable**
I – The Hilarious	**R – The Incredible**

S – The Unbeatable	**W** – The Magnificent
T – The Unstoppable	**X** – The Wonderful
U – The Epic	**Y** – The Amazing
V – The Mysterious	**Z** – The Undefeatable

Now, to find the second part of your codename look for the month that you were born in:

January – Zappy	**July – Zip-Zap**
February – Sparko	**August – Vroom**
March – Zing	**September – Pew-Pew**
April – Electro	**October – Gigatron**
May – Charger	**November – Turbo**
June – Buzzo	**December – Whoosh**

Put the two parts together and ta-da! You've got an imagineering codename fit for an epic adventure.

 # IMAGINEER TRAINING ID CARD

Now you can create an imagineer ID card.

Draw your own! Fill in your new imagineering
codename and answer the questions.

 ## DEPARTMENT OF SPARKOLOGY
IMAGINEER ID CARD

Codename:

What energises you?

How do you like to save electricity?

Favourite electrical thingy:

Superpower:

Secret weakness:

Take a look at mine if you need a zap of inspiration!

DEPARTMENT OF SPARKOLOGY
IMAGINEER ID CARD

Codename:
Captain Kilowatt

What energises you?
YOU DO! I love tackling a tricky mission with friends!

DEPARTMENT OF SPARKOLOGY
IMAGINEER ID CARD

How do you like to save electricity?
I like to use dark mode online AND I close all the doors and curtains to keep the draft out and keep the heat in when it's cold! Brrr!

Favourite electrical thingy:
My electro-thinga-bob-a-doo-hicky, of course!

Superpower:
Being able to ZOOM in to see the nitty gritty details and ZAP myself anywhere in a BLINK using my imagination!

Secret weakness:
Forgetfulness! Sometimes I forget to ask for help. I also forget to charge my phone! I also overshare! And I get distracted when I'm halfway thr–

pew-pew!

CHAPTER TWO
EVERYDAY ENERGY

How are you feeling? Energised? Ready for action? Buzzing for adventure?

Or are you feeling tired? Drained? Zapped of energy?

When was the last time you ate?

What did you eat?

More importantly . . . WHY did you eat?

Will I ever stop asking questions and tell you what all this is about?

Yes. Yes, I will.

I ask WHY you ate because it relates to the reason for this WHOLE BLINKIN' MISSION.

The reason WHY we eat is to get nutrients and ENERGY. If we're going to save the whole blinkin' planet from an ENERGY EMERGENCY, we should probably get straight what energy even is.

Energy is the capacity to power things. It's what makes everything do the doings!

For you and me, we get our energy from the food we eat. When you're hungry it might feel like an ENERGY EMERGENCY, but the one we're *really* focusing on in this mission is a different type of energy emergency. The two sources of energy at the centre of our emergency are electricity and fuel.

By ELECTRICITY, I mean what powers and charges all our electrical devices.

By FUEL, I mean stuff like petrol and diesel that we use to power most transport, including cars, buses, trucks and planes.

The universe of energy stretches far beyond that, but these types of energy sources are the ones we're here to get into the nitty-gritty about and are the ones that have been causing big blinkin' planetary problems.

Let's start by getting up close and quizzical with everyday electricity.

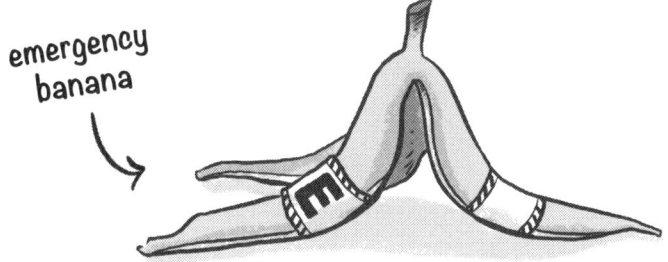

emergency banana

EVERYDAY ELECTRICITY

To be successful in our mission, we'll need to sharpen our senses. Being an imagineer means looking at the world through different eyes and seeing things that others don't.

Open your blinkin' eyes. Energy is all around us. Electricity is everywhere!

In this chapter you'll learn:

★ Some places electricity exists in nature

★ How to spot electrical things in your everyday life

★ What happens when you flick a light switch.

SWITCH ON

Electricity powers the things we switch on and off, and swipe and tap, and plug in and power down every single day. But is it so everyday that we have stopped seeing the electricity in our lives?

Let's get that brain of yours warmed up with some quick questions. Switch on to the world around you.

* How many things can you see in the room around you that use electricity or run on batteries?

* Is there anything near you that you can switch off to save electricity?

* Where do you think electricity comes from?

* Where do *you* get the energy you need to learn, play and grow?

Write down the answers in your imagineering notebook. You can even add more as you notice them later.

☆ ☆

NATURE'S ELECTRICITY

☆ ☆

Did humans invent electricity?

We did, in the same way we invented water. Which is to say we DIDN'T actually invent it at all. It already existed in nature, but we DID invent new fun ways to harness it. For water that was water slides and super soakers! For electricity it was those colourful blobby lava lamp things . . .

Okay, so we might have invented more amazing and useful electronic thingamies than that, but you get the idea!

It's obvious to see where water is in nature – it's in rivers, lakes and oceans and it falls from the sky.

Can you think of where you might see electricity in nature?

Perhaps we should brainSTORM ideas . . .

Maybe you need a ZAP of inspiration . . .

Any guesses?

I'm talking about LIGHTNING!

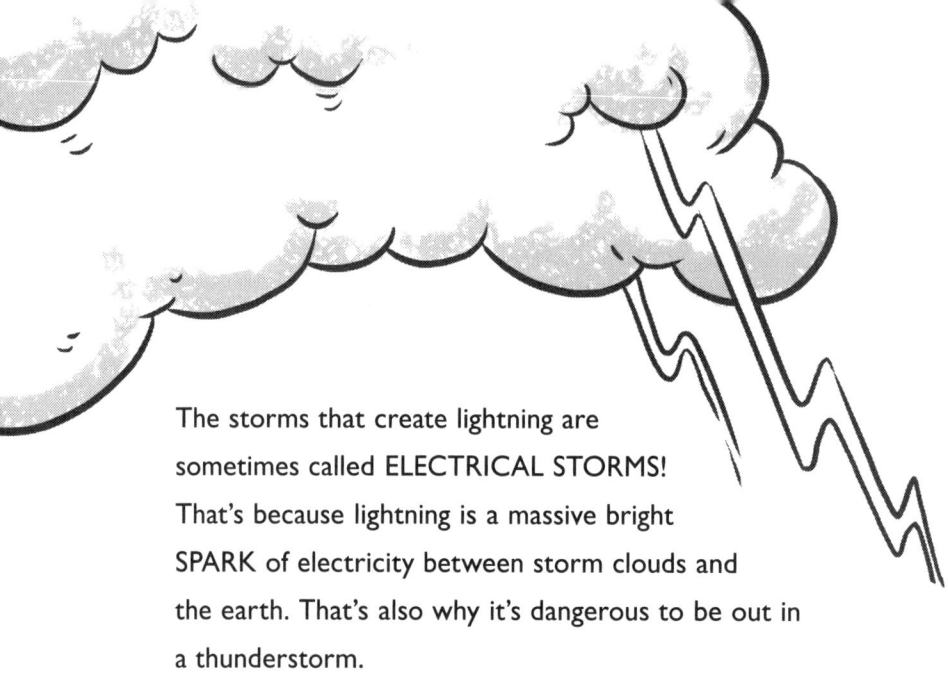

The storms that create lightning are sometimes called ELECTRICAL STORMS! That's because lightning is a massive bright SPARK of electricity between storm clouds and the earth. That's also why it's dangerous to be out in a thunderstorm.

FLASH FACTS

When you turn on the hot water tap, the water that comes out has been heated using energy – usually by burning gas (we'll get into more gas chat later) or by using electricity.

Around a quarter of household energy use is from heating water for washing dishes, warm baths, showers and washing laundry so you've got clean clothes to wear!

☆ ☆

EARTH HAS (GREENHOUSE) GAS!

☆ ☆

Peww! We've got a bit of a big stinkin' blinkin' gas problem on our hands here.

I'm talking about GREENHOUSE GASES – that's the pollution that floats into our ATMOSPHERE and causes the planet's CLIMATE to change.

Many things we do cause pollution (yep – even when we really care about the planet). When we burn different types of fuels like COAL, OIL and FOSSIL GAS (that's METHANE!) invisible gases float into the air.

The atmosphere is the layer of air that wraps all the way around the Earth. It's where clouds form and where birds fly. This layer of air keeps the world protected and it holds some of the heat from the Sun in, like a blanket. Unfortunately, those invisible gases I mentioned cause even more of the Sun's heat to get trapped in our atmosphere like adding extra blankets.

The extra blankets mean the planet is warming up, which really messes with our climate and weather. In different parts of the world the impact looks different. A warmer planet means more EXTREME WEATHER events, like droughts, floods, hurricanes and heatwaves.

★ What types of weather are there?

★ Can you think of a type of extreme weather event that has happened?

★ Why do you think they are called greenhouse gases? What is a greenhouse?

THE CARBON CYCLE

Any good mission starts with gathering all the background information we can get our hands on. For this one we need to go right down to the nitty-gritty basics – the building blocks of life itself. This information will come in handy on our quest to get our head around the problems and noodle on possible solutions.

Carbon. There's loads of the stuff. Everywhere! You and me and this book and everything in your lunchbox and the trees and the grass and the birds and, and . . . *breathe, Captain* . . . EVERY SINGLE other living thing on the planet are all what we call 'carbon-based'. You can find lots of carbon in the cells that make up our bodies. Non-living things like rocks and soil can also contain carbon as a main ingredient.

You know how eggs and milk and flour are all different ingredients, but you can put them together to make cake? Well, carbon is the key ingredient in LOADS of stuff on planet Earth.

Carbon is an element that contains ATOMS (the tiny little building-block ingredients that make up everything) that bond with lots of other atoms to make something new – like making a cake. But not . . . Wow, I really want cake now!

That's why carbon can be found in solid things like a diamond –
that's pure carbon that has been under a lot of pressure in the
ground – and it can also be found in $\underline{CARBON\ DIOXIDE}$ (CO_2),
which is a type of greenhouse gas floating around in the air.
Carbon gets around. Literally! In a cycle.

I present to you . . . drum roll, please . . .

I present t– Sorry, could you drum roll with a bit more ENERGY and PIZAZZ?

Thank you.

I present to you –

THE CARBON CYCLE

The crowd goes wild! Or they would if we had a crowd. I always forget to gather a crowd before I unveil the carbon cycle.

There are lots of places where carbon is stored and stays as an ingredient for millions and millions of years. But carbon is going through a constant cycle of change too.

Take a look at this picture of the carbon cycle. What do you see?

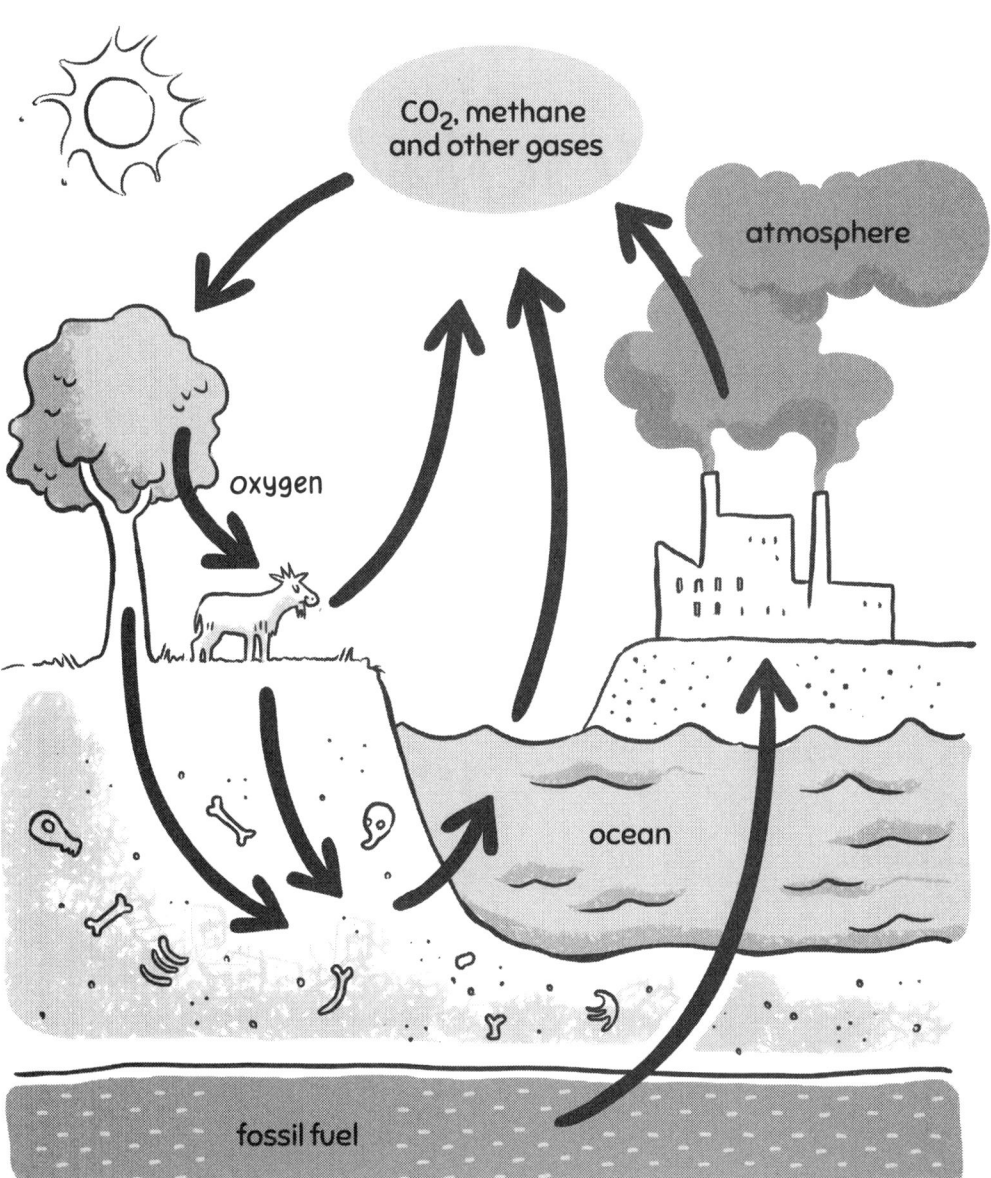

CO₂, methane and other gases

atmosphere

oxygen

ocean

fossil fuel

ZOOM IN

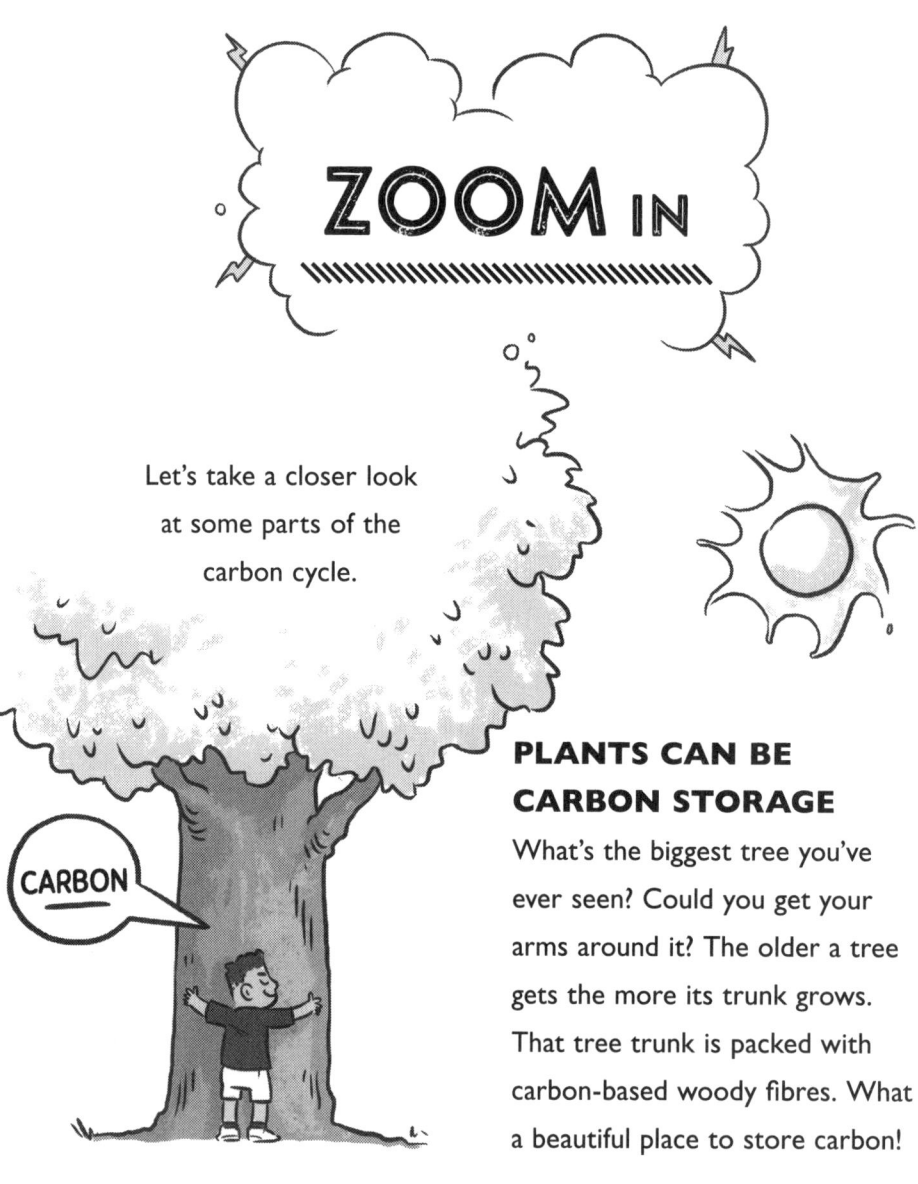

Let's take a closer look at some parts of the carbon cycle.

CARBON

PLANTS CAN BE CARBON STORAGE

What's the biggest tree you've ever seen? Could you get your arms around it? The older a tree gets the more its trunk grows. That tree trunk is packed with carbon-based woody fibres. What a beautiful place to store carbon!

LET'S GET CAUGHT UP IN THE FOOD WEB

Plants take in carbon dioxide through their leaves to make food, releasing oxygen in the process. This is called photosynthesis. The carbon that was part of the CO_2 in the air is now part of the sugars and cells in the plant that help it grow. When an animal eats the plant, it digests it so the carbon from the plant is used as energy for the animal – like me eating this banana I packed . . . yum. When plants and animals die, they are broken down by microbes, insects and invertebrates in the soil and become nutrients that can be taken up again by the roots of plants.

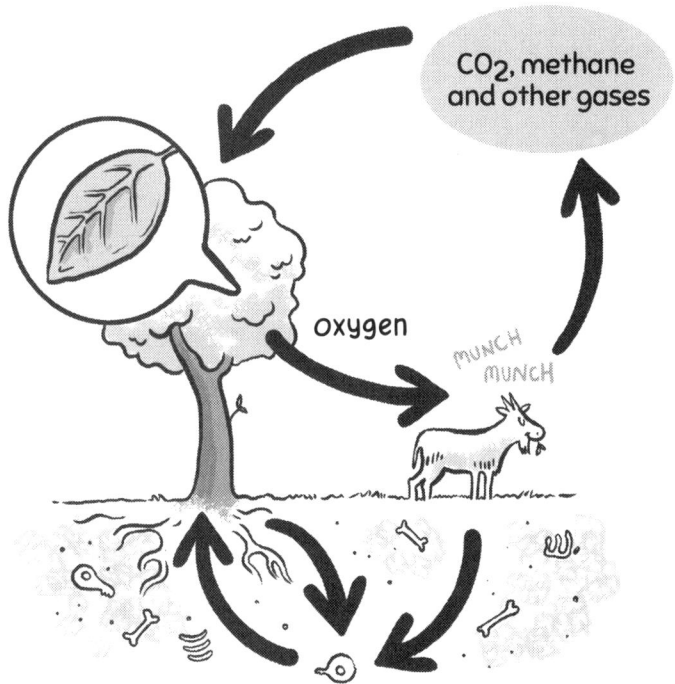

THE FOOD WEB IS JUST ONE PART OF THE CARBON CYCLE

Food is one of my favourite topics, but it's not the only possible path for a plant. If those plants we talked about earlier burned in a bushfire instead of ending up as food or decomposing in the soil, a lot of the carbon from those trees and other plants would go up in smoke, floating into the sky as carbon dioxide. Some of the carbon would also end up on the ground as ash.

You can see that there are lots of different possible directions carbon can take in this cycle and lots of different stuff that carbon could find itself as the main ingredient in.

OUR OCEANS ARE ALSO IMPORTANT IN THE CARBON CYCLE

There is a whole ocean-based food web, but our oceans also absorb carbon dioxide from the air. When carbon dioxide dissolves in the ocean water it forms carbonic acid. When the ocean water becomes more acidic, creatures like clams, snails, crabs struggle to make their shells.

Wait . . . remind me . . . what do shellfish and carbon dioxide have to do with electricity and our mission to save the blinkin' planet?

Well, since us humans have upped our electricity use, we have relied more and more on ways of making electricity that produce those greenhouse gases, including carbon dioxide, that warm the blinkin' planet. Oh yeah, AND acidify the oceans. Add that to the list. I've got one called 'Reasons Greenhouse Gases STINK' and it's why I filled up my last notebook so fast.

CLIMATE CHANGE AND EXTREME WEATHER

Another reason greenhouse gases blinkin' stink is – extreme weather, as I mentioned earlier. Greenhouse gases trap heat from the Sun in our atmosphere, warming things up for the planet. That's climate change. Things have been getting gradually warmer, not just in the atmosphere but in our oceans too. The temperature of our atmosphere and oceans drives our weather. Climate change is increasing how often we get extreme weather and how bad it is when we do.

WHAT'S EXTREME WEATHER?

That's a term used to describe a weather event that is out of the ordinary, has big impacts and is often really dangerous too. A few examples of extreme weather are:

* Flooding
* Drought
* Cyclones
* Blizzards

Can you think of any others?

Cyclones form over oceans and draw their energy from warm ocean water. The warmer the ocean water, the more energy a cyclone can get. That's why our warming oceans can lead to bigger and more dangerous cyclones or tropical storms forming in places where they may not have before.

How can climate change make both flooding AND drought worse?

On the one hand, higher temperatures can cause moisture to evaporate and dry out the soil making droughts worse. On the other hand, warm air can hold a lot more moisture so it can move this evaporated water to other parts of the planet causing major rainfalls and making flooding more likely.

WHAT ABOUT BLIZZARDS?

While there isn't much snow here in Australia, in other parts of the world snow falls every winter. A blizzard is a severe snowstorm and climate change can make them bigger. The high amounts of moisture that are held in a warmer atmosphere can freeze when the temperature drops in winter causing snowstorms that carry a lot more snow.

Climate change affects people across our big blinkin' planet in lots of different ways. And we've only scratched the surface!

If the way we make energy creates greenhouse gases, and those greenhouse gases cause climate change, and that climate change leads to extreme weather then . . .

We've got an ENERGY EMERGENCY on our hands! On the one hand, the way we make our energy isn't a good way forward. On the other hand, whatever type of energy we use we need to make sure we have enough for EVERYONE. This means saving energy AND changing energy.

A SHOCKING SCENE

How many things can you spot in this picture that use electricity?

Blink and you'll miss it! Learn to see things through an electrical engineer's eyes. Bonus: How many of these things use stored energy from a battery?

EVERYDAY ENERGY

64

SNAPSHOT

ELECTRONS – INVISIBLE EVERYDAY HEROES!

Every time you flick a switch to turn a light on, you're harnessing the power of an ELECTRICAL CURRENT to make the world (or at least the room) brighter.

Electrical engineering super-imagineers like me don't work alone. We rely on millions and billions and gazillions of invisible everyday heroes called ELECTRONS. After all, electricity would not even exist without electrons. Let me introduce you!

By flicking this switch on my electro-thinga-bob-a-doo-hicky here, we can shrink down to electron size in a flash. Hold on to your sockets everyone!

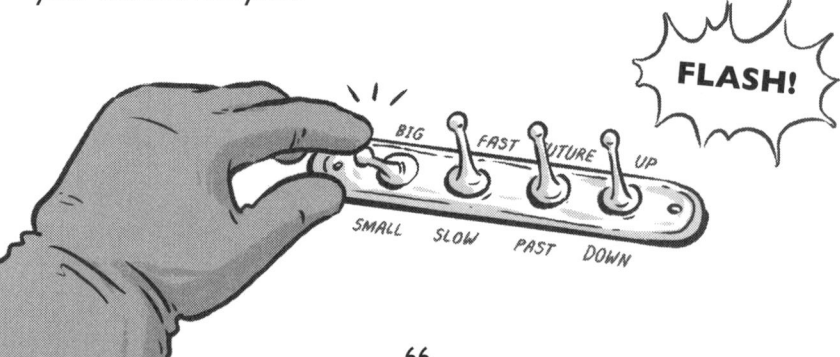

FLASH!

Still with me? All in one piece? Phew!

Electrons are busy buzzers. When the switch is flipped on, the electrons get excited and electricity flows like a river, causing the light to turn on. When the switch is flipped in the opposite direction, the electrons calm down and stop and the light goes out.

Let's zoom in and meet an electron.

Hello! Excuse me. Hi! Um . . . hello? Sorry, can we just . . . Oh dear. I forgot. The light is on. We'll need to stop the flow of excitement to get their attention.

Stand back, bright sparks! I'm just going to imagineer a little something . . . one, two, three, BLINK.

I redirected them to break the flow. Looks like it worked because the light has gone out.

Better switch on our torches.

Ah! Much better!

Hello! We're electrical imagineers. We come in peace. Tell us about yourself, little guy.

Hello there! Lovely to meet you, Buzz. Electricity can be dangerous for us (that's why I wear insulated safety gloves), so we didn't want to get too close while you were busy making a light shine. Buzz is one of many electrons that flow through the FILAMENT in an old-fashioned incandescent light globe or the LED in a modern energy-efficient light globe to make them glow.

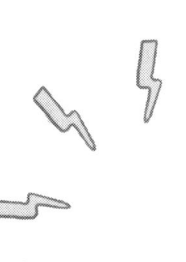

FLASH FACTS

Every second, millions and billions and
trillions of electrons flow through a
light globe while it's on. The energy
they give off makes it glow!

GET ⚡ ACTIVE

Scan the QR code for a bonus virtual multiple-choice activity.

A SHOCKING TALE

Have you touched a doorknob and felt a ZAP to your finger?

Have you rubbed a balloon on your head so that it makes your hair stick out and follow the balloon around?

These are both examples of static electricity!

The zap happens when your body has more electrons floating around than the thing you touch (like the doorknob). Electrons like to keep things nice and equal so they jump from you to the doorknob, and that evens out the electrical charge.

Rubbing a balloon on your hair causes some electrons to move from your hair to the balloon. When it comes to electricity – opposites attract! Now that your hair has fewer electrons than the balloon, it is pulled toward the balloon.

SAVING POWER TO SAVE THE PLANET

If my electro-thinga-bob-a-doo-hicky is right, this place is using loads of electrical power right now. Surely we don't need to use this much energy!

The more energy we use, the more of those greenhouse gases we talked about get created. And at times of the day when EVERYONE is using more energy for things like cooking, heating or cooling, this can put extra strain on the electricity network.

Put your imagineering goggles on and get that brain buzzing because it's time for your first shot at imagineering. Let's see if we can imagineer this place into using less electricity.

Shut those eyes tight, turn the page and blink three times . . .

BLINK FORWARD

I can't believe my blinkin' eyes! Are you seeing this?

You did it! We did it!

With our brainwaves combined we've imagineered a whole new world.

What do you blinkin' mean, 'It looks the same'? Clean your goggles, mate! You've gotta look at this with those imagineering senses we talked about.

Look at the electro-thinga-bob-a-doo-hicky. We're in the green!

SPOT THE DIFFERENCE

Let's take a closer look and see what's changed
around here. See if you can spot the difference
between these scenes opposite and the ones
on page 64 to find out why our
energy use has gone down so much.
Turn the page to find out more.

How many of these changes did you spot?

★ The curtains were closed. This helps keep the inside at a constant temperature without using extra heating or cooling.

★ Devices are unplugged when not in use.

★ Door snakes appeared. This stops draft from outside air.

★ Only one room needs to be heated or cooled. (And a cat's energy is keeping someone's lap warm!)

There are also some other changes around this place that are harder to see

★ Insulation in the roof stops the outside heat getting in during summer and the inside heat getting out in winter.

★ The incandescent light bulbs were replaced with more efficient LED ones that use much less electricity to light the room.

☆ ☆

AN ENERGY
SUPER-VILLAIN

☆ ☆

That's a really good start! But there's a glow in the corner over there that's telling me we have an uninvited guest in town . . .

How long has *she* been here?

Look . . . I'm going to level with you. You don't become an electrical engineer superhero who specialises in imagineering and saving the whole blinkin' planet without making a few enemies along the way.

PHANTOM POWER and I don't see eye to eye on energy use at all.

Name: *Phantom Power*

Superpower: *Sapping extra energy out of electronics.*

Weakness: *Disappears when appliances are switched off at the wall.*

Let me tell you a bit about her.

Well, well, blinkin' well. We meet again! I'd recognise that evil glow anywhere. Come out here, Phantom, and show your face.

(I'll keep her distracted with witty banter while you switch the console off at the wall.)

Think you can come into our living room and live off our wasted energy? Think again! I'm gonna zap you into next week. This will be the last time you mess w–

What's that? Oh . . . she's gone.

Nice work! You did it!

We've achieved a lot together
so far. You know, you just might
make it through Imagineering
Academy after all.

Phantom Power is a piece of cake, though, compared to some of
the other nasties ahead. But let's not dwell on that now. It's time
for some curious questions so you can level up.

LIGHTNING QUIZ

1. What are the tiny, invisible, charged particles called that flow through electrical wires?

2. What's one way you can keep the heat in your house during winter to save electricity on heating?

3. What should you do with electrical devices when you're not using them?

4. What is the name of the energy sucker we just defeated?

Flip to the Answers section on page 223 to see how you scored.

LEVEL UP

Congratulations! I thought you were a bright spark before, but you just got even brighter!

We're another step forward on our mission to save the whole blinkin' planet by imagineering new energy futures into existence.

Ready for the next challenge? Great! Follow me.

CHAPTER THREE

THE CLIMATE CULPRITS – FOSSIL FUELS

So, the plug goes in, the switch goes on and those electrons whiz around electrifying our electronic things and making them work. Simple, right? But this supply of energy must come from somewhere . . .

Where does the stream of ELECTRICAL CURRENT begin? They're interesting words, 'stream' and 'current'.

It's called an electrical current because it FLOWS, just like water.

Could electricity be like a river, do you think? And each electron like a single droplet?

Is there an ocean of electrons out there somewhere that feeds into our homes somehow?

Well, not exactly . . . but it is a fun thought experiment!

Water droplets seem to act a bit more wildly than our orderly friends the electrons. Drops of water slip and slide around each other a lot.

Water also doesn't need to be in a CIRCUIT to flow like electricity does – water can flow from one place to another, but electrons have to be in a loop to flow.

Scratch that thought!

It's fun to let the mind wander onto ideas even if the path doesn't lead us to the correct answer.

Much to ponder, bright spark. And much to learn.

In this chapter you'll learn:

★ Who or what is responsible for blinkin' stinkin' up the planet with FOSSIL FUELS

★ Where fossil fuels come from

★ Different uses for fossil fuels.

SWITCH ON

So, we've zoomed right in, met an electron and seen for ourselves how the flow of these tiny buzzers powers our electrical thingamies. But if you're thinking there's more to this story, you're right. Sometimes you need to zoom OUT to see the bigger picture. The first stage of the innovation cycle is thinking, so let's put our thinking hard hats on and let our minds muddle over a few quizzical questions:

★   Where do you think electricity comes from?

★   How do you think we get those electrons buzzing?

★   What can you do to save electricity?

★   Why is saving electricity good for the planet?

It's okay if you're not sure of the answers. Write your guesses in your imagineering notebook. You can come back at the end of this mission and see how much you've learned.

FLASH FACTS

Coal mines are the biggest source of fossil gas emissions in Australia. The gas escapes off the coal as <u>FUGITIVE EMISSIONS</u>!

ELECTRICITY – THE ORIGIN STORY

Where in the blinkin' world does electricity come from?

Well, I can tell you, but you have to promise not to tell no one. No, I don't mean you can't tell anyone. I mean **don't** tell *no one* – tell EVERYONE!

Part of why I'm telling you all this is because I hope you'll share this imagineering knowledge with the entire blinkin' planet! Or at least anyone who'll listen.

You know what? How about I show you instead of just telling you.

If my calculations are correct (which they usually are) we just need to get down to the power point, squeeze into the wires and then ZAP along the flow of electrons.

Put your detective hat on and hold onto your tool belts, everyone! We're following the electron trail all the way back to the beginning to see where it all starts.

 We're in! In a second, we'll pop out of the roof and follow the <u>POWERLINES</u>.

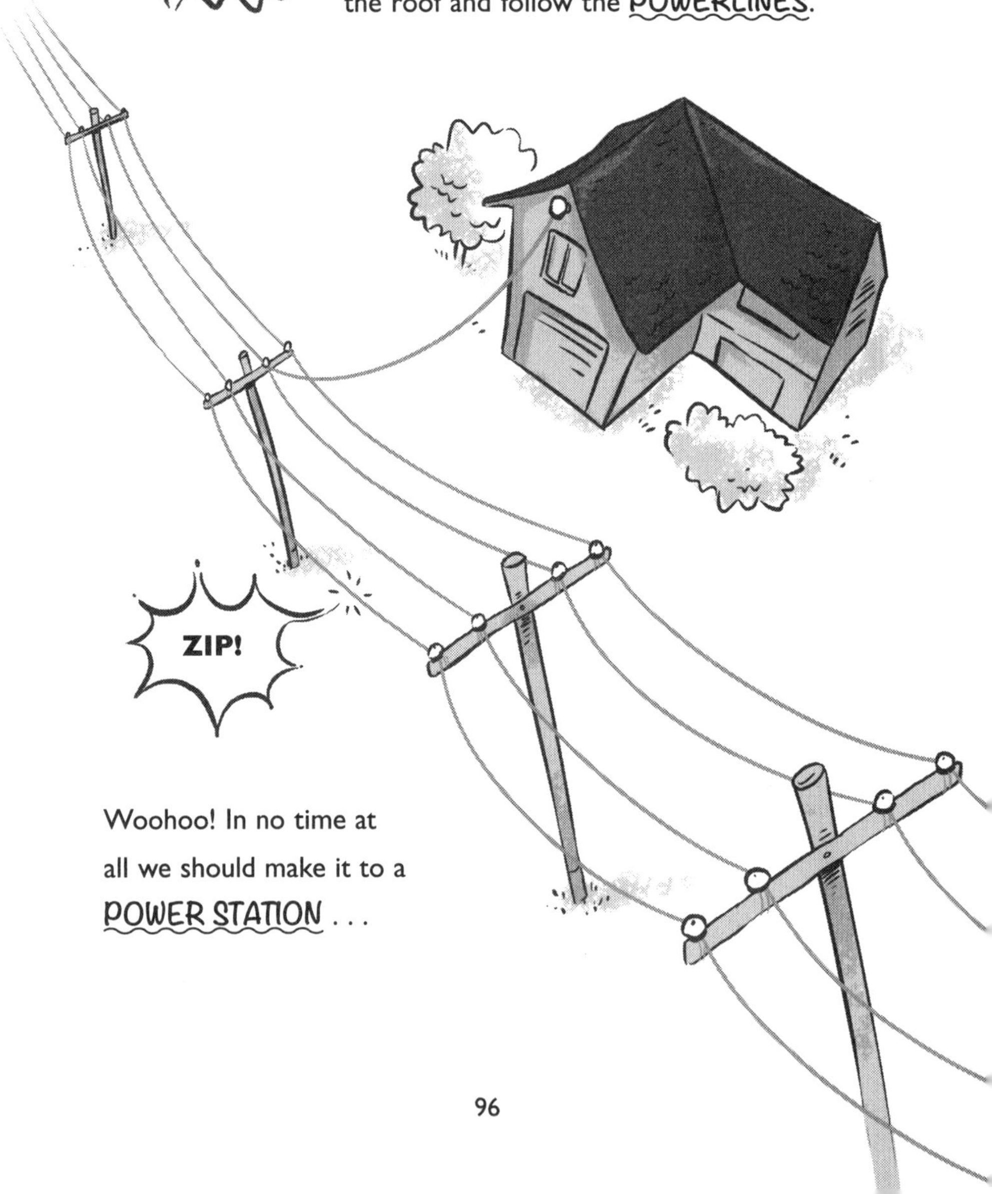

ZIP!

Woohoo! In no time at all we should make it to a <u>POWER STATION</u> . . .

WHOOSH!

There it is, which means –

Weeeeeeeeee!

Plop.

FIND THE
ENERGY SOURCE

We're almost there! Follow the powerlines back from the
house, until you discover the energy source. What is it?

ZAP!

SNAPSHOT

Ah! As I was just saying, we're at our destination. Welcome to the power station.

This is one of many power stations that are feeding electric power in the form of buzzing electrons into the powerlines and off to homes, schools, streetlights, sports stadiums and more.

This one is powered by coal.

What's that and what does it have to do with electricity? I'm glad I asked!

FROM COAL TO CURRENT

Coal is a type of black or brown rock that comes from the ground – we'll get to how it got there in a minute. Coal is dug up by machinery at coal mines and transported here. It's then crushed up and burned. Heat from the burning coal is used to boil water and – just like you might have seen when the kettle boils – the boiling water creates steam.

The steam pushes a <u>**TURBINE**</u> and the spinning turbine powers a <u>**GENERATOR**</u> that excites those electrons, creating the electric current that powers our homes.

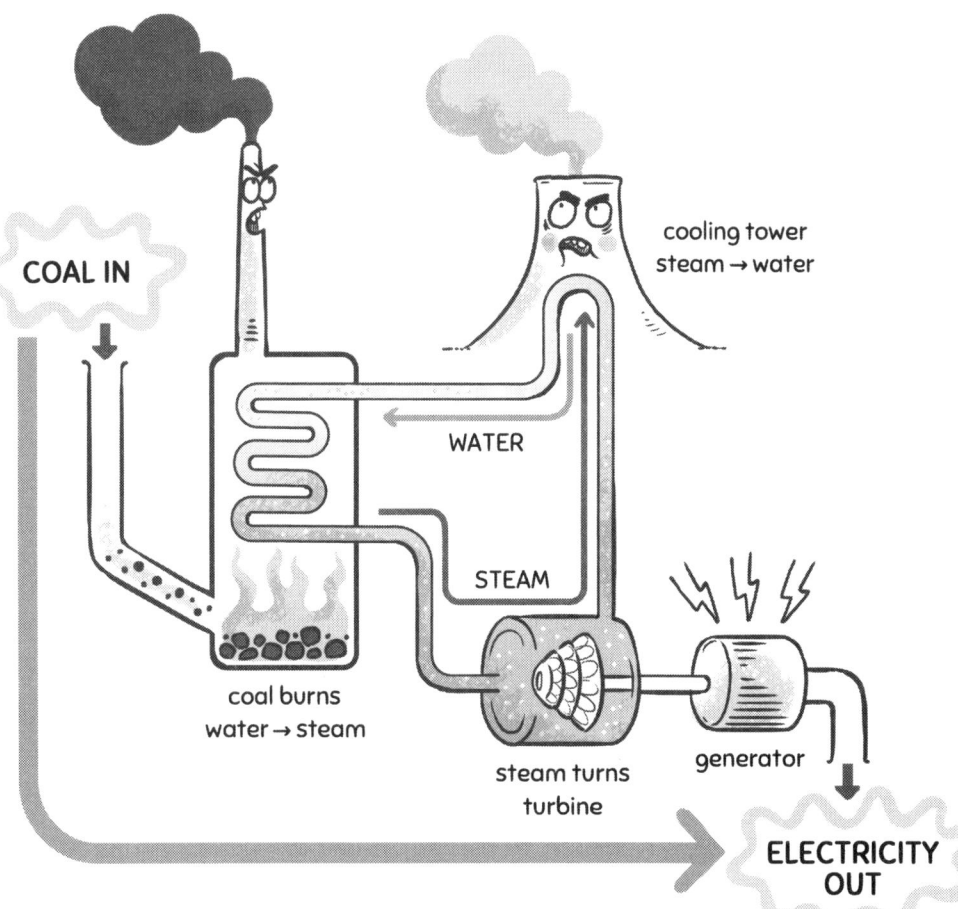

COAL IN

cooling tower
steam → water

WATER

STEAM

coal burns
water → steam

steam turns
turbine

generator

ELECTRICITY
OUT

It sounds like magic. But it's science.

So what's the big blinkin' problem, you say? Coal goes in. Electricity comes out.

Look, mate . . . do I really need to remind you of the mission here? We're here to save the whole blinkin' planet! Of course, there's a blinkin' problem.

Let's weigh up the pros and cons of burning coal for energy.

The good news: Lots of technological advancements have come from people using coal to create electricity, like computers and the internet. There are also people (including engineers like me) who work at coal mines, so they provide jobs for lots of different people.

The bad news: Burning coal creates carbon dioxide – that's a greenhouse gas. We talked about them earlier. The OVERSUPPLY of greenhouse gases going into the atmosphere is why we need to save the blinkin' planet in the first place – they're heating it up too blinkin' much.

AND that's not to mention extreme weather events becoming worse AND more frequent, AND ocean acidification from all that carbon dioxide mixing with seawater and making it harder for shellfish to make their shells! Won't SOMEBODY think of the SHELLFISH?

Sorry . . . *deep breaths* . . . I am very passionate about the mission and sometimes I get carried away. Where was I? That's right. I was just about to tell you the super bad news.

Are you sitting down? You might need to for this.

The truth is coal isn't the only climate culprit we're up against in this mission to save the whole blinkin' planet from GREENHOUSE GASES.

That's right, coal isn't acting alone. And carbon dioxide isn't the only greenhouse gas we need to worry about either.

I'm glad you were sitting down because we shouldn't stand for this!

I mentioned earlier that coal comes from the ground. So do the other climate culprits we need to combat. These nasties go way back. To explain who they are, I need to start by telling you their origin story.

FLASH FACTS

Eunice Newton Foote was a scientist and inventor in the 1800s. She was the first scientist to warn that rising carbon dioxide levels in the atmosphere could impact the climate. She did an experiment where she put one thermometer in a glass cylinder that had carbon dioxide pumped into it. And she placed a thermometer into another glass cylinder that had air (which is a mix of different gases) pumped into it. She put both cylinders into the sunlight. The one with carbon dioxide in it got a lot hotter! This demonstrated for the first time what we would come to know as the greenhouse gas effect. Wow! What an amazing imagineer she was!

FROM FOSSILS TO FUELS

The three climate culprits – including coal – are part of a gang called the FOSSIL FUELS. This name is full of clues about where they came from.

Let's break it down.

Have you ever heard of a fossil?

fossil

/ˈfɒsəl/ (say 'fosuhl)

noun a fossil is a special rock that has an imprint of something that lived on Earth a long, long time ago. Palaeontologists study fossils to learn about everything from plants and insects to dinosaurs that once roamed the Earth.

What about the word fuel?

fuel

/fjul/ (say fyoohl)

noun a fuel is something that is burned to release energy.

Hundreds of millions of years ago, this beautiful blinkin' planet of ours looked very different to how it does today – it was covered in massive swamps. As plants and other living things died in the swamps they sank right down to the bottom. Over millions and millions of years, dead plants and animals and dirt formed more and more layers at the bottom of the swamps. These layers became heavier and heavier over time as more dead stuff, dirt and water was added on top.

These heavy layers became hot and pushed down so hard on the dead plants and animals below that they changed into coal.

That's why we call coal a fossil fuel – it's literally something that formed from plants and animals that lived a long, long time ago. Most of the coal that we use is even older than the dinosaurs!

It's not just coal that formed over those hundreds of millions of years. The downward pressure and heat of these layers of dead plants and animals, dirt and water also formed two other types of fossil fuels deep in the ground:

★ Gas

   and

★ Oil

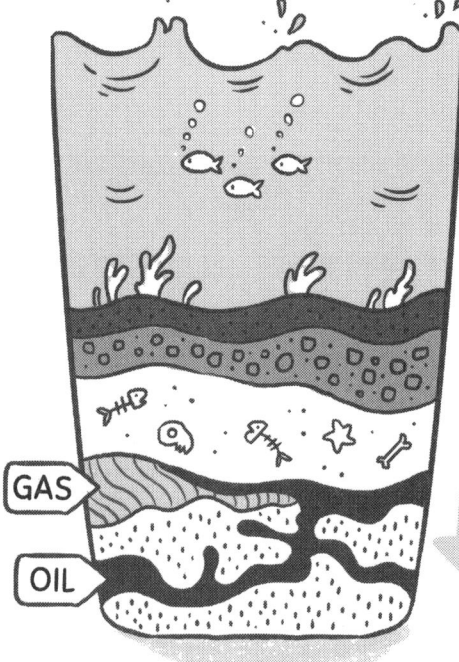

GAS

OIL

TIME AND PRESSURE

These fossil fuels share an origin story, but what else do coal, oil and gas have in common?

Well, they have all been super useful since humans discovered them. And they're also behind this greenhouse gas problem. In fact, fossil gas even has gas in the name.

Together they are the three main climate culprits. Here – I put together some info, so you'll know these fossil fools if you see them!

THE THREE CLIMATE CULPRITS

The three main culprits behind the planet's problems are on the loose. When coal, oil and gas were deep in the Earth's crust they were minding their own blinkin' business.

Digging them up and using them for all kinds of things seemed like a clever idea at first . . .

I guess those engineers couldn't predict that we'd be where we are now.

Name: Coal

Last seen: Being ground up and burned to make electricity. A special type of coal is also used for making steel.

(UN)WANTED

Name: Gas

Also known as: Fossil gas or natural gas

Last seen: Cooking food on the stove. Making electricity. This gas is even used in the creation of fertiliser!

(UN)WANTED

Name: Oil

Also known as: Crude oil or petroleum

Last seen: Fuelling cars and making plastic. It can also be used for heating and for making electricity! Chemicals in oil are used in hundreds of other products too.

GAS ON THE RUN

Methane and carbon dioxide are both gases with the same key ingredient – carbon. The gas we use in our homes and power plants is mostly made of methane, which is a big greenhouse gas baddie. Do you remember why? That's right, it's because when there's a lot of it in the atmosphere, it acts like a giant greenhouse, trapping heat in the Earth's atmosphere and impacting temperature and climate across the whole blinkin' planet. Methane really heats things up for planet Earth.

Gas is a master of disguise because it's invisible and has no smell! But there are clues when gas is around.

You might think – but I've smelled what gas smells like when it gets turned on for cooking on the stove or at a BBQ. Well . . . that smell you sniff if there's gas about was actually ADDED to it so that we can tell if there's ever a gas leak. The added chemical is called mercaptan. In fact, the smell that gets added to the gas is the same foul-smelling stuff that can be found in that OTHER type of everyday gas – our farts! Did someone fart or is there a gas leak around here?

You might have seen a blue flame on the stove heating up a pot of food. That blue flame is gas burning.

Gas is piped up from the ground below and captured so it can be burned like this. But a big problem is when the gas sneaks past the pipes and makes a getaway out into the atmosphere to join the other greenhouse gases. Gas is an escape artist! It's very good at it.

These runaway gases are called fugitive emissions. Remember them? Other fossil fuels are involved in gas getting away too. When humans dig up coal or extract oil, this gives gas that was trapped underground with it the perfect opportunity to escape. In fact, coal mines are the biggest source of fossil methane emissions in Australia. I told you these climate culprits are in this together.

OIL

When oil is pulled up from underground it's a mixture of lots of different chemicals.

Some of these chemicals are used to make fuel for cars and other vehicles that get us from A to B. Petrol and diesel are types of fuel that power many of our cars, buses, trucks and motorbikes. When the car is turned on, the fuel gets ignited by a spark to push a series of pistons that power the engine and make those wheels go round. The more a car is driven, the more of the fuel gets burned, which is why you need to go to the petrol station to refuel. The burning of petrol or diesel in the engine changes the fuel into lots of different polluting gases including greenhouse gases. Carbon dioxide is the main greenhouse gas that comes out of a car's exhaust pipe, but it's not the only one. Greenhouse gases and other pollutants go out the exhaust pipe at the back and – you guessed it – up into the sky!

I mentioned only SOME of the chemicals from oil are used in these engines. What else do we make using chemicals from oil?

A big one is PLASTIC!

Look around. How many different things can you see right now that are made of plastic?

Just think . . . how many things in your life wouldn't exist if it weren't for countless organisms being buried, liquified and slowly transformed under layers of earth and water for millions and millions of years before they were found and pulled up out of the ground? What a long, drawn-out journey it is to become a lunchbox!

This is also a good reminder of why our big blinkin' fossil-fuel problem stretches outside our mission. Plastic waste is another big stinkin' problem that you can read about in the book, **How to Save the Whole Stinkin' Planet**. See more about that book at the end of this one! Other eco-heroes are out there tackling that planetary problem head on, too.

So now you've met the big three!

We can't let these climate culprits get away with spreading greenhouse gases.

Do you know what time it is? Oh, thank you! I forgot to charge my phone.

Okay, apart from what's on the clock, it's time for a . . . drum roll, please . . .

LIGHTNING QUIZ

Phew! There's nothing like a lightning-fast brainstorm to build those brain muscles. What do you mean the brain isn't a muscle? Oh, wow . . . I didn't learn that at Imagineering Academy. Thanks! Speaking of lightning speed, it's time for a lightning quiz.

1. What are the three types of fossil fuels that I like to call the climate culprits?

2. Why are they called fossil fuels?

3. How long did it take for fossil fuels to form? Months, years, hundreds of years, or hundreds of MILLIONS of years?

4. Why is using fossil fuels so blinkin' bad for the planet?

Remember to turn to the Answers section on page 225 to check how you went.

IMAGINEERING TIME

Before we blink ourselves into one of our many possible futures, we need to focus. Sometimes the problem seems so big that it helps to break it down into smaller parts.

Let's zoom in on just one of the three culprits here: oil.

Remember that oil is turned into petrol and used to fuel a lot of our cars and other forms of transportation.

This time when we blink forward, let's try something new!

Let's try some rapid-fire brainstorming. We're going to blink quick and think quick to imagineer lots of wild and wonderful ways we can get around without burning petrol.

It's okay if they are like something we've seen before. It's okay if they are something completely new that has never even been thought of.

Brainstorming can be a key to unlocking creativity. Where there's a brainstorm, there's brain lightning, right? What sort of imagineer would you be if the Imagineering Academy didn't teach you that?

On your marks . . . Get set . . .

BLINK FORWARD

BAM! It's a motorbike powered by the wind!

POW! It's a plane flying by plant-power! And a helicopter powered by the Sun!

ZIP! It's a . . . what IS that? I'm not sure, but all ideas are welcome and, whatever it is, it looks like it can seat twenty people, five dogs and a cat and is powered by a team of . . . super-strong cyber-butterflies?!

Wow . . . now THAT's some creative blinkin' thinkin', bright spark!

ZAPPEEEEEeeeee! It's . . . it's . . . oh . . . wow . . .
it's just the three of us biking and walking.
Sometimes great options are right under
your nose and you don't even realise!

Okay, one more! For those longer journeys we've got . . .

YAHHHHHH! An amphibian boat-bus powered by . . . let's see . . . what's the fuel?

Oh, I see. It a fuel that turns food waste into engine food. That's clever! Nice work.

Got more ideas? Great! Write those down or draw them in your notebook. You never know when a wild idea might come in handy.

GET ⚡ ACTIVE

Scan the QR code for a bonus test of your climate culprit knowledge!

LEVEL UP

Well, I said we'd come across a lot nastier nasties than the phantom we met at the start of our training, and they don't come more terrible than that trio! Coal, oil and gas might be climate culprits but there was a time when they were seen as energy heroes. That's why they've ended up everywhere now.

Knowing what you're up against is half the battle. And I'm proud of you for how far you've already come as a budding imagineer.

Give yourself a pat on the back and then tighten your tool belt for the next chapter.

CHAPTER FOUR

OUR SUPERPOWERS – RENEWABLES

Are you still with me, bright spark? I know the planet's problems can seem like scary things to overcome, but this adventure isn't only about the big blinkin' problems like those climate culprits – it's about GINORMOUS blinkin' possibilities.

Fossil fuels have had their part to play in our history and when we first started using them – long before you or I arrived on the scene – we didn't know what we know now about the downsides. But since figuring out the problems, lots of clever imagineers have been coming up with some exciting solutions that I'm looking forward to telling you all about.

You know what they say about knowledge.

Oh . . . you don't?

Well, knowledge is power. In fact, it's a SUPERPOWER!

And I've only just begun to share this power with you.

In this chapter you'll learn:

★ The difference between RENEWABLE and NON-RENEWABLE energy

★ More in-depth information about how burning coal produces electricity

★ How electricity is made with three different renewable energy sources.

SWITCH ON

You know the drill, bright spark. We need to shift that brain of yours into gear before we plunge into our next imagineering challenge. We've got to switch from problem mode to solution mode. Maybe you've already got something in mind.

Here are a few questions to warm up your brain:

* How do you think we could replace fossil fuels?

* Where else do you think we could get energy from?

* Is there anything on Earth that doesn't run out when you use it?

* Can you think of any solutions to our fossil-fuel problem?

Write down your answers in that imagineering notebook of yours because any one of them could be a seed that sprouts a bigger idea.

Asking questions is the first step to finding answers, so let's get to it.

SNAPSHOT

Meeting the gang of climate culprits sure brings home the problem that we are trying to tackle on this mission. Each one of them plays a part in putting greenhouse gases into the atmosphere when we use these fossil fuels to power our everyday lives. Saving the whole blinkin' planet from greenhouse gases is going to help us make the climate safer and healthier for all of us.

Apart from all the greenhouse gases they make when we burn them, there's another problem with using fossil fuels. Can you think of what it might be?

When we burn fossil fuels for energy, that's it! They're gone!

Turning a fossil fuel into electricity, petrol or even stuff like plastic means that it's gone and we can't use it again. It's a great disappearing trick and we're very good at it, which is why we have had to keep searching for more and more coal, oil and gas to feed the world's hunger for electricity and other fossil-fuel-based stuff.

But we humans have already dug up and drilled a lot of the coal, oil and natural gas that the Earth has been keeping safe, and it hasn't been magically replaced. That's a superpower no one has!

It took millions of years for these fossil fuels to form, after all. We're not going to see new fossil fuels replace everything we've dug, piped and drilled up overnight. We're using them far too quickly for that.

FOSSIL FUELS CAN'T BE RENEWED

Renew is a word worth zooming in on.

The letters 're-' are at the start of lots of words to show that something is happening again.

For example, when you replay a video, you are playing it again.

You can't spell **renew** without **new**, either, so you can think of the word renew as meaning 'making something new again'.

RENEWABLE VERSUS NON-RENEWABLE

Since fossil fuels – coal, oil and gas – can't be renewed, we call them non-renewable. And the energy we make from these fuels is called NON-RENEWABLE ENERGY.

Energy made from things that we can renew (things that don't run out no matter how much we use them) is called RENEWABLE ENERGY.

Can you think of some things that might be renewable? Write down your ideas in your notebook.

If you can't, that's okay. When we met the climate culprits, we imagineered a future where there were new types of energy that don't cause the big blinkin' problems that fossil fuels do.

Renewable energy might just be the answer!

Overcoming phantom power and the electrical waste we faced at the start of your mission was as simple as using less energy and switching electronics off when you don't need them. That helps a lot to combat wasted electricity, ensure there's enough energy to go around and reduce our fossil-fuel use.

But combating our need for non-renewable, greenhouse-gas spewing fossil fuels requires some serious superpowers! And renewable ones at that.

Renewable-energy sources are all around us. From the wind in your hair to the Sun shining down on us, even flowing water and waves in the sea can be used to make electricity that doesn't cause such a blinkin' mess.

How can we use wind, water and the Sun to make electricity? Let's take a closer look and find out.

138

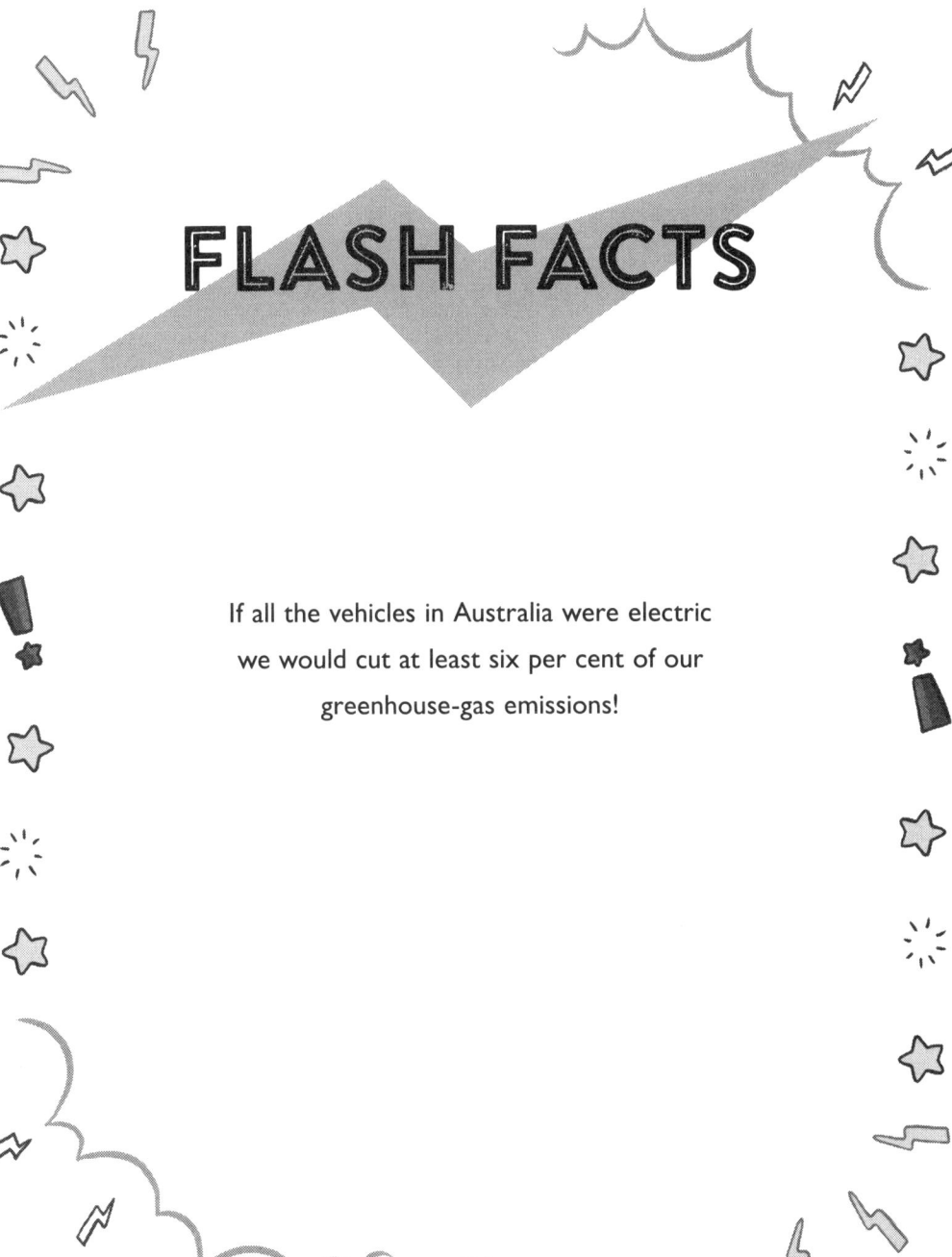

FLASH FACTS

If all the vehicles in Australia were electric
we would cut at least six per cent of our
greenhouse-gas emissions!

NON-RENEWABLE ENERGY RECAP

How is electricity made when we burn coal? (Or fossil gas for that matter?)

First, let's recap to refresh our memory. But this time we'll zoom in on the process even more than before to get a closer look.

Making electricity is all about changing one type of energy to another.

1. Ground-up coal is burned to make heat energy.

2. Heat energy is used to boil water to make steam that rises. That's called moving or kinetic energy.

3. This moving steam turns a turbine – another type of moving energy.

4. That turbine powers a generator – yep, more movement!

The generator has a spinning magnet on the inside and coils of wire on the outside. Spinning the magnet on the inside excites the electrons and generates electricity in the coils of wire. And there we have it – electrical energy!

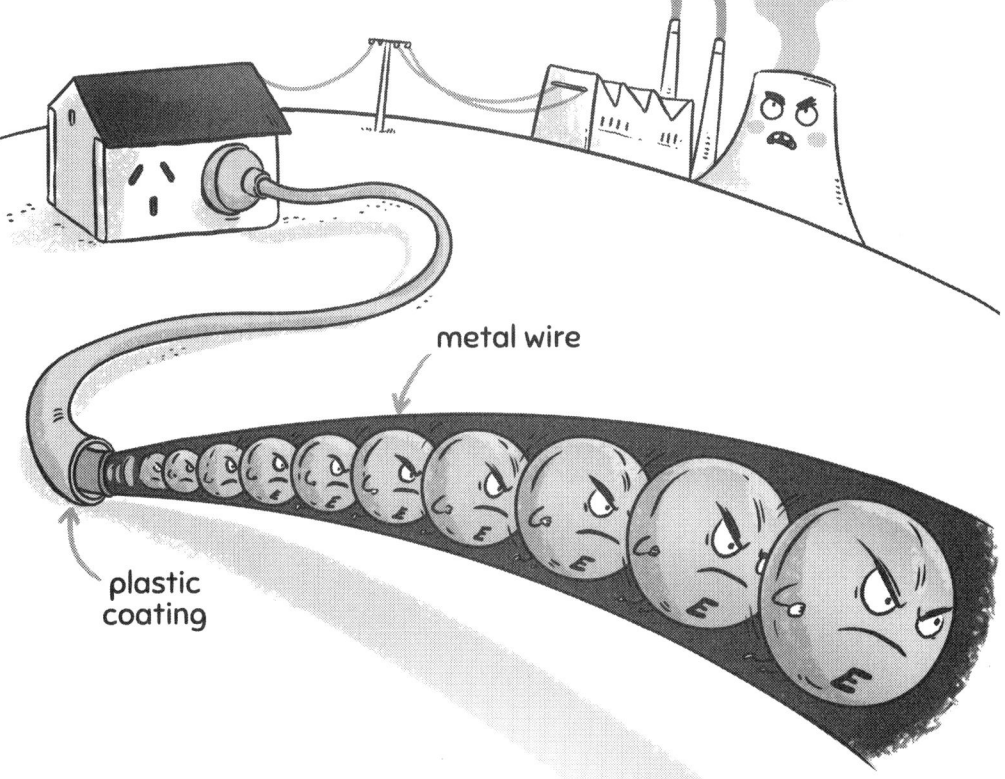

metal wire

plastic coating

So, the fossil fuel – coal in this case – was only needed at step one as a fuel to burn to boil the water.

★ Can you think of something else we might do to replace any of these steps?

★ What else could we burn? Is your idea something that's renewable or non-renewable?

★ Are there pros and cons (good and bad sides to your idea)?

I hope your pencil is sharp because we'll be giving that imagineering notebook a good work out. Don't be afraid to poke holes in your own ideas. That's how imagineers find the best solutions!

I'm just going to have another emergency snack while you brainstorm. Want some? It's raisins and . . . what's that? Oh, that's tool-belt fluff . . . No? Okay, more for me!

Once you're done with your brainstorming session, turn the page and I can show you a few ingeniously imagineered solutions.

We need something that is:

1. Renewable

2. And can make electricity.

That's called your 'criteria'. As you grow as an imagineer you might want to add more criteria to your list like cost, materials, locations and other considerations, depending on the project at hand. Let's work with just these two for now.

WIND POWER

The first renewable energy candidate I want to introduce you to is wind.

No, I don't have wind! Well . . . not right now. I mean THE wind.

> 1. **Is it renewable?** Yes. Just because you use <u>WIND POWER</u> doesn't mean it runs out. Some locations are windier than others though!
>
> 2. **Can it make electricity?** Also, yes!

Here's how . . .

To harness the power of the wind, engineers have designed special wind turbines. The wind pushes on the blades, making them spin – that's moving or kinetic energy, without having to burn anything!

This turns a shaft inside – more moving – which powers a generator. And the generator (as we talked about earlier) is what turns this movement into electricity.

The innovation cycle must have been really spinning when engineers designed these wind turbines. They had to consider the number, the angle and the shape of the blades to get them spinning just right. Wind turbines are also engineered to turn even when there is only a light breeze – that's why you might have seen them turning even when it's not super windy.

WATER POWER

Next up – water power, also known as hydropower.

Even before humans were making electricity, we were using water as a renewable energy source.

Ancient humans across the globe have used flowing or falling water to turn large wheels called – you're not going to believe this – a waterwheel. One popular use for waterwheels was for powering mills that crush grain to make flour.

river flow

What about our current-day needs?

1. **Is it renewable?** Yes. Around two thirds of our planet is covered in water. Water is renewable.

2. **Can it make electricity?** Also, yes.

Here's how . . .

Falling or flowing water can spin a turbine to power a generator too. Instead of burning coal or gas to make steam to spin a turbine and power a generator to make electricity, hydropower uses the movement of liquid water to do it instead.

Note: We need to use fresh water for this because salty seawater rusts equipment.

<u>DAM</u> – that's a big dam!

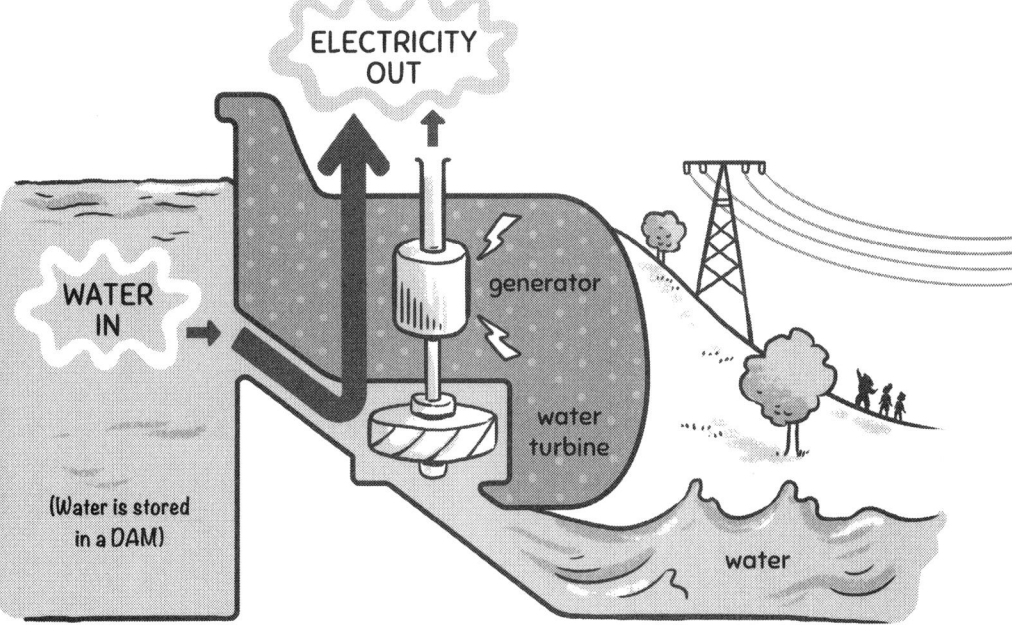

Today <u>HYDROELECTRIC</u> plants are set up on dammed waterways. Why? Well, even though water is renewable its constant flow isn't always something you can depend on. The dam wall is used to control the flow of the water so that there can be a more reliable supply of electricity. Phew! You don't want to be about to finally beat the most difficult level of your game when the power cuts out.

But building a dam to control water availability means that we humans are changing the way water flows down a river, which can be a big problem for the wildlife that has relied on the river to survive.

Downstream of a dam, the river might receive less water. While upstream a lake begins to form, flooding the banks, drowning plants and forcing animals out of their homes.

It's a problem that needs us to put our thinking caps on.

Maybe it's something you'd like to learn more about and even imagineer some solutions for!

SOLAR POWER

I've saved the biggest till last. THE SUN! That big ball of heat and light in the sky.

Our planet is orbiting around it constantly. No matter what happens today, I can guarantee you the Sun will rise again tomorrow.

Electricity that is made using the power of the Sun is called SOLAR POWER.

1. **Is it renewable?** Absolutely. There's no way any humans could possibly use up all the Sun's energy.

2. **Can it make electricity?** Also, yes. And in a bit of a different way to the methods we've discussed so far.

Have you seen a solar panel?

Sometimes they are on rooftops of houses and businesses. Sometimes they are out in fields surrounded by sheep on a solar farm. (I suppose if there are sheep there it must be a sheep farm too!) There are even solar panels in SPACE on SATELLITES.

Solar panels are flat shiny sheets designed to collect energy from the Sun and turn it into electricity we can use.

Go on. Ask me how.

I'll tell you anyway . . . Solar panels are made up of lots of small sections called solar cells and are positioned to face the Sun for as much of the day as possible. Solar cells are made with a really

thin layer of a material called silicon. Glass and sand are mostly made of silicon too. This silicon layer is where the electrons come from. When sunlight hits the cells in the solar panel, it knocks an electron from each atom of silicon free. This creates a flow of electrons and the electrical current that results from that can be used to power our homes.

What? No turbines and generators? Nope. None. Pretty clever imagineering, right?

FUTURE FARMING

Sheep, cattle, fruits, grains and vegies are all things we're used to seeing on a farm. But did you know you can farm energy too? Solar farms and wind farms are paddocks of solar panels or wind turbines where renewable energy is made. Some farmers even combine these different types of farming by growing a crop under the wind turbines or grazing sheep under solar panels.

Not all energy farming happens on land, though. It can get pretty windy out at sea! Offshore wind farms generate energy from wind turbines in the ocean. The electricity they make flows back to power stations on land through underwater cables. The great thing about farming wind at sea is that the winds out there are so strong that they can make even more energy than wind farms on land.

BLINK FORWARD

I hope those three savvy solutions got your brain buzzing with possibilities. Now let's put our brains together and imagineer what a fully renewable future could look like.

BLINK! Wow! Look around. This place looks totally different! Well . . . not TOTALLY different. It looks like we've still got a lot of the things we have now but . . . different.

Are the roofs around here looking . . . shinier? They're made of what? Wow . . . there are so many solar-powered innovations you've imagineered I don't know where to start. All this renewable energy will bring our planetary warming problem under control!

Why is that bus so quiet? It can't be . . . It's run on renewable energy too? I guess that's why the petrol stations look more like charging stations now. Hmmm . . . this is something we'll investigate more later.

Are these windows double-glazed? I'm so glad you remembered those energy-saving tips we learned about earlier. That's going to save so much energy for heating and cooling. You really have thought of everything.

Wait a blinkin' second! Just how far forward into the future did we blink ourselves?

Surely this is fifty years ahead.
Or a hundred?
Let's check.

Oh. Oh my . . .

We've hardly moved! By this stage you might be a bit taller and need a bigger-sized set of imagineering boots, but if my imagineering calculations are correct, this is a lot sooner than even I thought and may already be happening today.

I've tried this experiment before on my own, and it has never turned out THIS well. It looks like we make quite the team.

There's something about this imagineered future that's special and might be just what we've been looking for. I can't quite put my finger on it . . .

WORKING TOGETHER

That's it! Every time I've tried to imagineer ways to combat climate culprits on my own, I could only focus on one small part at a time.

Using renewable technologies is a superpower, but the piece of this puzzle that I've been missing is the one we've found here – PEOPLE POWER.

The most important part of any engineering project is cooperation and sharing a goal, and that's what our brains combined have imagineered here. We want a future where no one gets left behind, after all, so it makes sense that we need to work together.

No wonder this vision of the future has us delivering our planet-saving goals on such a speedy schedule.

GET ACTIVE

Scan the QR code and test your superpowers!

FLASH FACTS

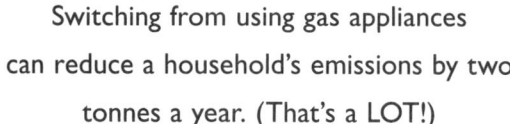

Switching from using gas appliances can reduce a household's emissions by two tonnes a year. (That's a LOT!)

Cooking with gas is responsible for up to twelve per cent of childhood asthma in Australia. That means cutting it out would benefit the planet AND our health too – double win!

LIGHTNING QUIZ

1. What does it mean if something is renewable?

2. Are fossil fuels – coal, oil and gas – renewable or non-renewable?

3. What is one type of renewable energy we can use to help power the planet?

4. Is it better to cooperate with each other as a team or try to tackle all the planet's problems at once as a lone ranger?

Remember to turn to page 226 to check your answers.

LEVEL UP

I can't believe it, bright spark! Except I absolutely CAN believe it . . .

You've just levelled up AGAIN. That means we're nearing the end of your training. Let's recap on our Imagineering Academy adventure so far.

You were briefed on the mission at hand – to save the whole blinkin' planet. (No pressure!)

We learned about the basics of electricity and about the planet's greenhouse-gas problem.

Phantom power reared its energy-sapping head, but we defeated it in the blink of an eye!

We came face-to-fossil-fuel face with the climate culprits themselves – coal, oil and gas. And we found out about the exciting possibilities of renewable energy from wind, water and the Sun.

We harnessed the power of knowledge, brainstorming and PEOPLE.

And here we are. Ready for whatever comes next, which I'll show you in a FLASH.

CHAPTER FIVE

IMAGINEERING OUTSIDE THE BOX

When you learn about a problem and find a solution, it's tempting to think, That's it. Job done. Mission accomplished. Time to go home and hang up the hard hat. But before we get carried away with the solutions we've already imagineered, I want to introduce you to a bunch of other cleverly engineered solutions that are out there. Since this is a global problem, it means we need global solutions and different things will work better to combat the climate culprits in different places, and with different criteria and considerations than the ones we have already talked about.

Let's see what happens when we imagineer outside the box. These aren't just ideas in the design and test phases of the innovation cycle either – these are engineered energy solutions that are out there making a difference right NOW.

In this chapter you'll learn

★ The different ways that fossil-fuel-free electricity is being made around the world

★ How batteries work and why they are important.

I'm curious to hear your thoughts on what our next adventure has in store.

★ Apart from the Sun and the wind – what other things might give us renewable energy?

★ How can we store energy to use later?

★ Why do you think some energy solutions might work well in one part of the world but not in another?

★ Are there any planet Earth problems we might not have even talked about yet?

Write those answers down. Better still, take a moment to look back on your last brainstorming sessions. Got any wild ideas that you think might be on this list of innovative solutions?

Let's find out.

SNAPSHOT

This mission has really put you through your paces, bright spark. Not only have we got up close to some big blinkin' greenhouse gas problems, but we've also identified the three main climate culprits – looking at YOU, coal, oil and gas! AND we got the lowdown on three of the heaviest-hitting renewable-energy superpowers on planet Earth: wind, water and the Sun.

So far, Mission Sparkology has been a glowing success.

Just as your brainstorms have been filled with ideas raining down from your brain to the page and flashes of brilliant brain lightning too, the engineers and imagineers of the world have also come up with LOADS of renewable energy solutions.

If you truly want to master this mission and ace Imagineering Academy, you've got to think outside the box – and even outside this country – even MORE.

We've only just started to scratch the surface of cleverly imagineered inventions that are out there already powering the planet in a greenhouse-gas-free way. Let's zip around the world and zoom in on a few examples.

GEOTHERMAL POWER

Let's zoom over to Aotearoa, New Zealand! This area is in the Taupo Volcanic Zone where they are harnessing GEOTHERMAL ENERGY.

Let's break that word down. 'Geo' means the Earth and 'thermal' means heat.

Geothermal

/dʒioʊ'θɜməl/ (say jeeoh'thermuhl)

adjective of or relating to heat emanating from the molten core of the Earth.

When the Earth formed it was super hot, and the core of the Earth is still SUPER hot today! The outer layers of the Earth — the mantle and the crust (the ground under our feet) are wrapped around the hot core at the centre.

But the heat from the Earth's core does escape toward the surface sometimes. It can even break right through the crust, creating formations like volcanoes and hot springs.

The volcanic zone in Taupo is home to a *LOT* of those little escape hatches for geological heat. When the heat from kilometres underground comes to the surface, it can be harnessed to boil water, creating steam. This means engineers can use it to . . . do what?

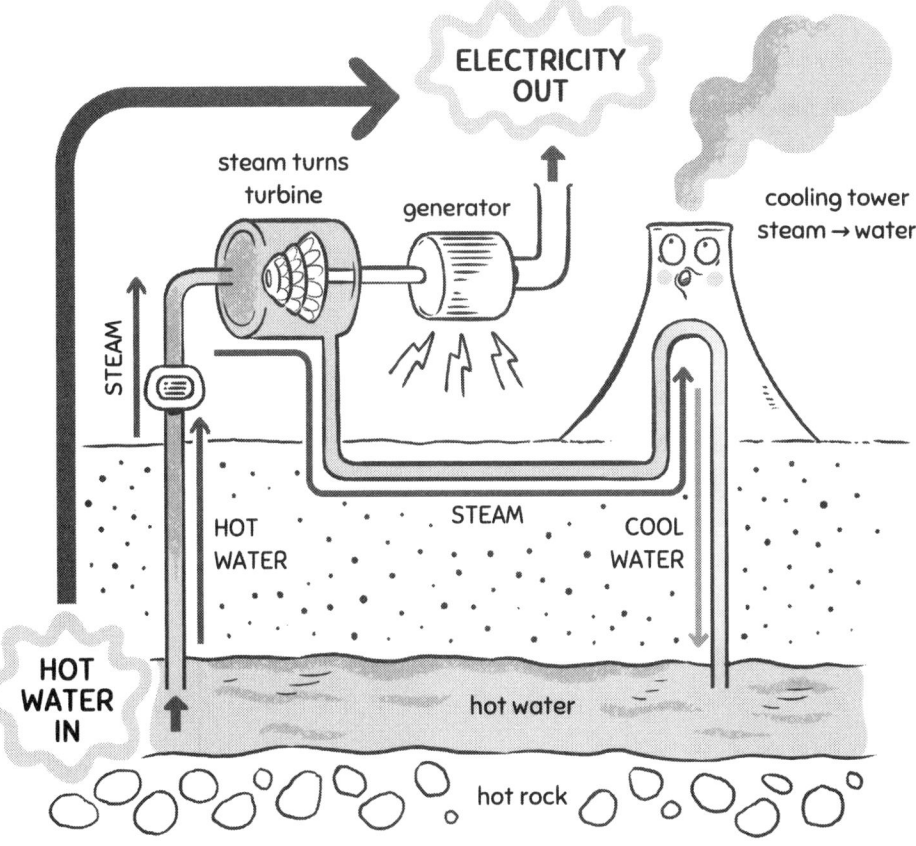

Yep – you guessed it! To spin a turbine to power a generator that excites some electrons to make electricity. Sounds familiar, doesn't it?

On the other side of the planet in Iceland geothermal energy is being put to use too. Many people in the Icelandic city of Reykjavik keep warm using geothermal power. Even through the icy cold winter (the country is named ICE-LAND after all). Lots of people use this power to heat their water too.

Pros: No greenhouse gases. It's also very cheap to run and it's renewable – the Earth's core isn't cooling down any time soon.

Cons: Many places – unlike New Zealand and Iceland – don't have hot rocks close enough to the surface to make geothermal power an option or those hot rocks aren't close enough to the places where energy is needed.

Okay, next!

NUCLEAR

To see the next outside-the-box way to make electricity, we need to travel to France. Which means I just need to grab this handle on my electro-thinga-bob-a-doo-hicky and . . .

FLASH!

Voila! We're here. See that power station down there? It's a bit different from the ones we've seen so far. That's because France gets most of its electricity from NUCLEAR ENERGY. What's that, you ask? Well, of course I'm BUSTING to tell you.

Nuclear energy is yet another way to make steam that (say it with me now) spins a turbine to power a generator that excites some electrons to make electricity.

Nuclear power plants like this one get that heat from a special process called FISSION. But before we learn about fission, we need to talk about ATOMS.

UP AND ATOMS!

Atom? Where have we heard that word before?

I mentioned at the start of this mission that the element carbon contains types of atoms. Take a look at the Glossary at the back of this book if you need a reminder about what atoms are.

And what was the element used to make solar panels?

That was silicon. It might sound silly, but that's made of other SERIOUSLY useful types of atoms.

Atoms are tiny little bits that make up everything on Earth – including you and me and this book and that pigeon and that truck and those flowers and this cloud and my sandwich and . . . oh, yes . . . all the fillings on my sandwich . . . and . . . what was I saying? Sorry, I got distracted by my lunch. (I need fuel to power my body, after all.) Anyway, the point is that everything is made of tiny parts called atoms.

THE ROCKSTAR OF THE NUCLEAR-ENERGY SHOW

The element used in nuclear power plants is a big heavy-metal element called uranium. It turns out heavy metal isn't just a type of music. Rock on! Speaking of rocks, although there are no nuclear power plants in Australia, there ARE mines where uranium gets dug up out of the ground and transported overseas to power plants just like this one.

THE VISION FOR FISSION

Do you remember the electricity-making electrons that we met at the start of this adventure? Well, electrons whizz around the outside of atoms. And it's quite easy for them to shift from one atom to another.

The really important thing about atoms, when it comes to nuclear power, is that the parts that make up the centre of each atom (protons and neutrons) are held together really tightly with a lot of force.

It's REALLY hard – almost impossible – to pull the centre of an atom apart.

That's where a process called FISSION comes in.

178

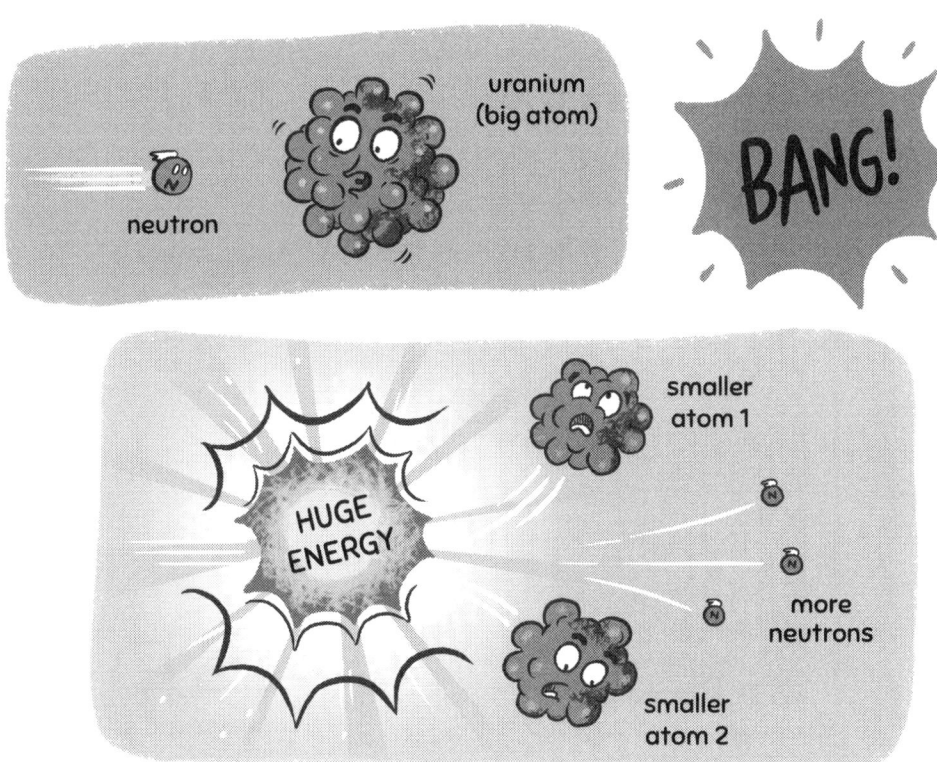

In nuclear reactors, scientists fire a stream of atom parts (neutrons) at the big uranium atoms to split them apart. When the core of the uranium atom bursts apart it releases loads of heat energy – and more neutrons. That's fission. This process can be repeated again and again to keep creating heat until there are no more big atoms left and the show's over (at least until more uranium comes to the party).

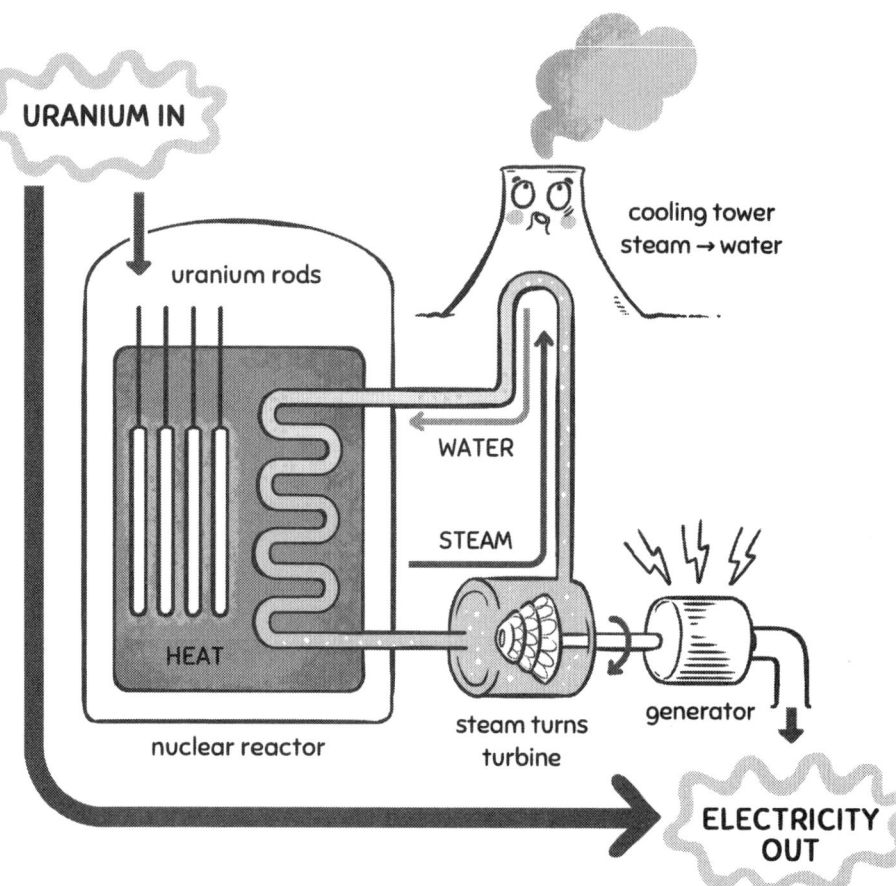

The heat from fission is used to boil water and create steam, which turns a turbine, which powers a generator that . . . yep – produces electricity. You must be seeing a pattern by now!

Pros: No greenhouse gases. And it uses very small amounts of the energy source (e.g. uranium).

Cons: This process produces nuclear waste that is dangerous to humans and the environment so needs to be very carefully and securely stored for a long, long time before it's safe. Nuclear reactors are also very expensive and take a long time to make, so if (like Australia) you need greenhouse-gas-free energy ASAP and you don't already have one of these, it might not be the best option.

Okay, THAT'S IT! That's ALL the types of ways to make electricity that exist on planet Earth . . .

. . . is what I WOULD say if we HAD talked about ALL the types of ways to make electricity that exist on planet Earth. But the TRUTH is . . . that's NOT all of them! There are more energy solutions that HAVE already been invented. There are also improvements and changes and varieties of the energy solutions we've already talked about, and I am almost CERTAIN there will be more clever people imagineering even more ways to create electricity in the future too. Maybe you'll be one of them! Maybe there's the first spark of an ingenious energy idea in your notebook already.

☆ ☆ ☆ ☆ ☆ ☆ ☆ ☆ ☆  ☆ ☆ ☆ ☆ ☆ ☆ ☆ ☆ ☆

FINDING PROBLEMS IN OUR SOLUTIONS

☆ ☆

Imagine we've decided that, for where we live in the world, our best options are to use wind and solar power. That means when the Sun shines on those solar panels and the wind turns those wind turbines, we're making electricity.

But . . . what about . . . and I don't want to scare you so come closer because I'm going to whisper this . . .

What about . . . when the Sun doesn't shine and the wind doesn't blow?

GASP!

I know, I know. Our solution seemed so perfect. Did I blinkin' ruin it?

Deep breaths . . . I've trained for this . . .

If I've learned one thing at Imagineering Academy, it's that finding potential problems with even our favourite solutions is an important part of the process. How are we supposed to imagineer a world we want to live in if we're not open to looking closely at our ideas, especially if there's something we don't like the look of?

Let's go back to the drawing board and give this problem a good hard thinking over.

WHAT IF THE SUN DOESN'T SHINE AND THE WIND DOESN'T BLOW?

If you're using geothermal power then you don't have to worry about the Earth's core cooling down all of a sudden when you're in the middle of watching a movie, but for some renewable power sources like solar and wind we can't generate electricity all day and all night long.

What if we're relying on the Sun for our power?

Sometimes it's cloudy and the sunlight will be blocked from hitting our solar panels. And even on a clear day the Sun will go down eventually.

What about wind energy?

Even in very windy places, the strength of the wind changes and it's not windy ALL the time.

What do you think we can do about this problem?

If only there was a way to make lots of power while the Sun is up or the wind is blowing, and then save it to use later when the Sun isn't shining or the wind isn't blowing . . .

I know! It was right at the tips of my blinkin' fingers all along . . .

Bright spark, there IS such a magical technology that allows us to do this. In fact, you've probably used it.

I'll give you a clue. You can find these in:

★ Gaming controllers   ★ Watches

★ Laptops   ★ Wireless computer mouses

★ Smartphones   ★ Torches

★ TV remotes   ★ Drones

Need ANOTHER clue?

It starts with 'B' and rhymes with 'schmatteries'.

YES! BATTERIES. How did you guess?

FLASH FACTS

The centre of an atom is called the nucleus and that's where the word nuclear comes from. Fission isn't the only type of nuclear reaction. There's also nuclear fusion. That's what happens when two atom centres (nuclei) combine to make one. This happens in the middle of stars, including the Sun. A lot of heat energy is released when nuclear fusion happens so that explains why the Sun is so hot. Scientists and engineers have been working on ways to harness this power to make electricity.

ENERGY STORAGE

Batteries are handy household energy storage units, and they are the perfect solution if you need to be plugged into power all the time.

I mean, imagine if we needed phones to always be plugged into the wall? Imagine how long the cord would have to be to go on a walk while FaceTiming Grandma! In fact, we might not even leave home with our phones if it weren't for batteries. We'd only use them at home in the room where they are plugged into the wall.

Actually, that's what everyone did before mobile phones!

The point is, batteries are blinkin' amazing.

We have lots of different shapes and sizes of batteries for different things. Some batteries can be taken out and recharged. Other batteries are built right into the device.

Everything from a watch – whether it's a smartwatch or an old-school watch – to a car, uses batteries. In fact, electric cars use batteries so they can get around without needing fuel made from fossil fuels. More on that later.

Batteries are renewable energy's best friends.

That's because the ability to store energy in a battery means that the battery can be charging up when the Sun DOES shine, and the wind DOES blow, so that energy can be saved to use later when there isn't enough sunlight or wind to make energy in an instant.

HOW DO BATTERIES WORK?

Think of a battery as an energy storage unit.

At each end are metal parts called electrodes. Inside the battery between these metal ends is a mix of chemicals. Different kinds of batteries use different mixes of chemicals. When a battery-powered device switches on, the electrons in this mix of chemicals flow out of the battery at one end and into your device to power it. And the electrical current flows back into the battery at the other end, completing the circuit.

The more charged a battery is, the longer it can be used before it runs out.

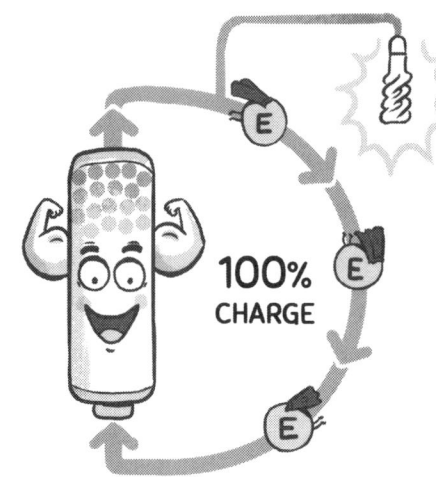

100% CHARGE

0% CHARGE

SAVING BATTERIES TO SAVE ELECTRICITY

The more you use a device that runs on a battery, the faster the battery will run out. This means it needs to be recharged or replaced more often.

The way you use your battery-powered device can also drain the power supply more quickly. Can you guess what the most energy-draining things to do on a phone are? Write down your ideas in your notebook.

What did you come up with? Here's what I got:

★ Having the screen brightness way up

★ Playing videos online

★ Using GPS for navigation

★ Playing games

★ Having lots of apps running at the same time.

These can make the battery run out much quicker, meaning you have to recharge more often – using more electricity. Now, brainstorm some ways you could make a phone battery last longer.

DON'T BIN YOUR BATTERIES!

Imagine you've been playing with your favourite battery-powered toy or game and it runs flat. You open the back to look at the battery and realise it's not the kind you can recharge. What do you do? Throw it in the bin?

NOT SO FAST! Batteries are pretty special – yep, even flat non-rechargeable ones. They contain lots of precious metals *and* hazardous substances like those chemicals we talked about. That's why it's important to dispose of them safely so they don't sit in landfill, heat up and become fire hazards.

Repeat after me: I don't want to be responsible for a landfill fire! Or a bin fire! Or a garbage truck fire for that matter.

I thought so.

You also don't want to miss the opportunity to have those precious metals recycled so they can be reused to make new batteries and other tech.

Luckily, there's somewhere we can take batteries to make sure the chemicals are safely taken care of and the metals are recycled: an e-waste collection point or battery store.

Phew, now we know we've protected everyone *and* done our best for the planet.

MOVING SMARTER

The great thing about running cars on electricity is that unlike petrol and diesel made from oil, which is a fossil fuel, the electricity used to charge EV batteries can be made without using fossil fuels. What is an EV?

EV stands for ELECTRIC VEHICLE. That's a car or other type of transport you can charge by plugging in to electricity instead of using petrol or other fuels to power it.

But electric vehicles aren't the ONLY answer when it comes to getting from A to B in a way that saves the planet. In fact, there are HEAPS of other options that put even LESS pressure on the planet. I'm talking about:

★ Public transport (electric edition) – electric buses, trains and trams are a great way to move lots of people in the same direction without all the materials, space and fossil fuel needed for lots of cars.

★ Getting moving – this includes walking and biking and is a wonderful way to exercise while costing the planet less. There's no pollution. The only fuel needed is your energy! And much less material is used to make a bike.

BATTERY BREAKDOWN

We know how batteries work, how to avoid running them down too quickly and how to dispose of them properly. But how do they help the blinkin' planet?

Batteries have been getting bigger (and sometimes smaller) and ALWAYS better over time, as more scientists and engineers put their brains together to make new ones. The uses for batteries have expanded too, thanks to these new types of batteries.

That's right, I'm talking about batteries for electric vehicles like cars, buses and even boats AND batteries for mass energy storage.

Could batteries be the answer? Does this mean it's not such a bad thing that the Sun doesn't always shine and the wind doesn't always blow?

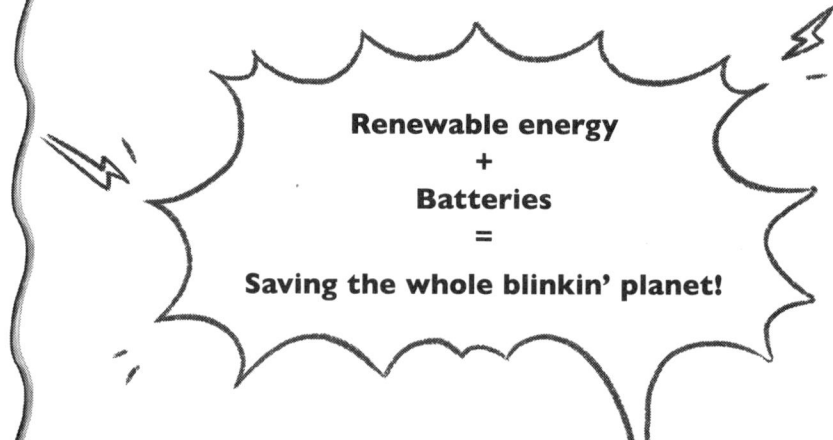

Renewable energy

+

Batteries

=

Saving the whole blinkin' planet!

FLASH FACTS

Water power has been around for a long time. Some of the earliest known hydropower inventions were created in China more than 2000 years ago. Waterwheels were used to power machines for milling grain, crush rocks at mines and process timber. Waterwheels were also used in the Roman Empire to grind grain by turning something they called a 'millstone'.

DOES THIS ADD UP?

Here are three places where batteries can make a big difference in saving the blinkin' planet by storing the renewable power from energy sources like the Sun and wind.

1. Residential batteries – these are batteries connected to homes so that the solar power generated on the roof can be stored during the day for use at night.

2. BIG BATTERIES – massive batteries attached to solar or wind farms to store power at a larger scale to supply a whole community.

3. Electric-vehicle batteries – whether it's single cars, or public transport like buses, batteries in vehicles allow them to charge up using renewable energy and then use that energy over time.

There's one more clever way to store energy that combines some of the ideas we have already talked about. Can you remember what it is?

Let's blink forward and take a look with our own blinkin' eyes.

Brains together. Let's think innovative energy-storing thoughts, bright spark.

3 . . .

2 . . .

1 . . .

BLINK FORWARD

BLINK!

Can you hear that?

It sounds like water flowing. This can't be hydroelectricity . . . we already talked about that.

Let's dive in and have a look.

Did you bring a snorkel?

Don't worry. I brought spares.

Hmm, it looks like this is hydroelectricity but with an exciting twist. If I'm not mistaken, this is PUMPED HYDRO ENERGY STORAGE.

Wooooo!

The crowd goes wild!

Mate . . . why am I the only one going wild here. You don't seem pumped enough for pumped hydro.

Follow that water. I'll explain everything on the way.

I mentioned we can use flowing or falling water to make electricity. This water sure is falling. Right now, we are flowing downhill from one water reservoir to another, which means we should get to the turbine soon. Hold on tight!

Weeeeeeeeeeeee! Phew!

Okay, as we whizzed through with the rest of the water, we turned the turbine to generate electricity, right? No surprises there. But . . . here comes the twist! It sounds like we're here right on time.

That sound is the pump starting. This system uses part of the electricity we just made to pump all this water back to the top again. Once we're at the top? Well, we're just energy waiting to happen all over again – like in a battery – and the cycle continues.

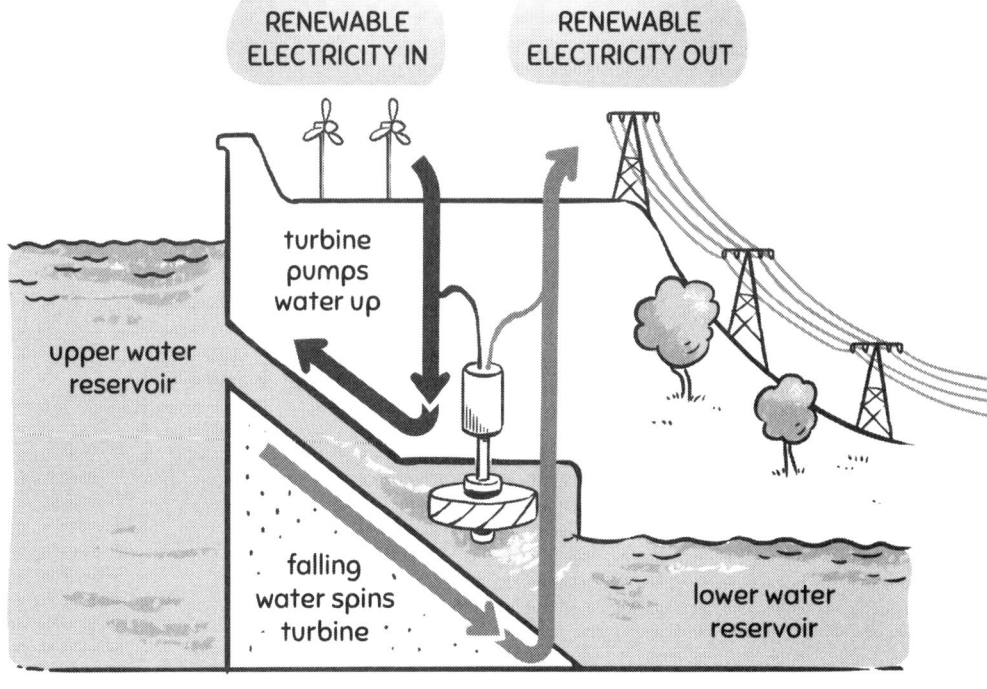

RENEWABLE ELECTRICITY IN

RENEWABLE ELECTRICITY OUT

turbine pumps water up

upper water reservoir

falling water spins turbine

lower water reservoir

How neat is that? We imagineered an energy-making battery made of water. This might just make enough energy to power a whole grid!

LIGHTNING QUIZ

Wowee, we've used a lot of brainpower! Let's take a seat and refuel. Did you bring your lunchbox? Don't worry, I always bring an emergency banana, remember? Rule number 4586 of Imagineering Academy is to always stop for snacks. How are you supposed to have the energy to explore the world of energy otherwise?

While we refuel our bodies and brains, let's treat ourselves to a quick quiz to recap.

Remeber to turn to page 227 to check your answers.

1. Where does the heat used in geothermal energy come from?

2. Where does France get most of its energy?

3. What technology helps to store solar energy when the Sun doesn't shine and wind energy when the wind doesn't blow?

4. What do hydropower and pumped hydro storage have in common? Hint: What does 'hydro' mean?

5. How's your banana? Are you going to eat the rest of that?

LEVEL UP

Bright spark, I have to tell you something. You have lettuce in your teeth. Okay, you got it.

There's something else I have to tell you. I'm proud of you. You've done it again. And I'm not talking about getting lettuce out of your teeth. WE'VE done it again! We just bounced around the world looking at different ways imagineers like you and me are working to save the whole blinkin' planet. You've not just completed this part of Imagineering Academy, you've utterly blown the entire thing out of the park!

There's only one thing left to do – GRADUATE AND CELEBRATE!

Oh, yeah . . . and we've got a whole blinkin' planet to save too.

CHAPTER SIX

GRADUATION

You're here! You made it! WE made it!

Was that really your first-ever electrifying imagineering adventure?

Wow, who knew? (I did, but you seem like an absolute pro!)

Our mission to save the whole blinkin' planet from GREENHOUSE GASES by stopping energy waste, combating fossil-fuel climate culprits and skilling up in the art of imagineering energy solutions has been a wild ride.

But you're so confident and brave and clever. I knew you were up for it.

Before you get to your emotional victory speech, I do have one last challenge.

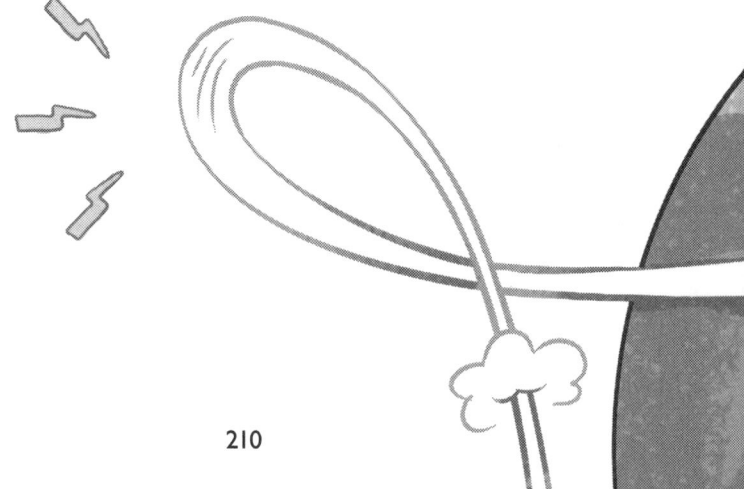

GRADUATION

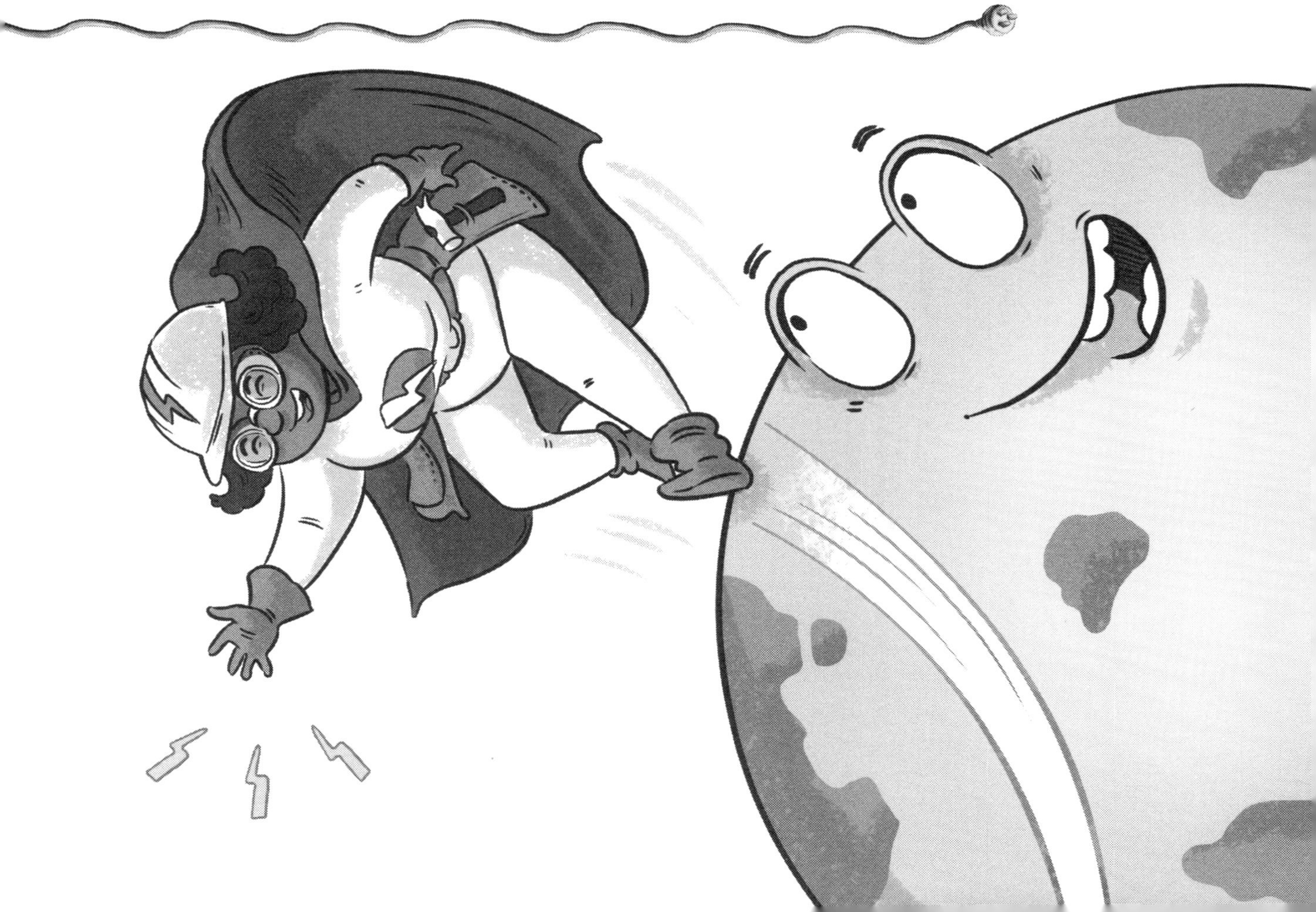

THE ULTIMATE QUICK-FIRE LIGHTNING QUIZ

It's a recap before we wrap! Two questions from each level of Imagineering Academy. You've already smashed them out of the park to be here. You've got this, bright spark.

1. What are the four stages of the innovation cycle?

2. What is a greenhouse gas?

3. What are the tiny invisible everyday heroes that make electricity possible?

4. What is the name of the eco-villain who saps energy from your electronics when you're not using them?

5. What does 'renewable' mean?

6. Name the three fossil-fuel climate culprits that create greenhouse gases.

7. Name two sources of renewable energy.

8. What important material is used to make solar panels?

9. Where can you store solar and wind power when the wind doesn't blow, and the Sun doesn't shine?

10. What is one important use for batteries that can help save the blinkin' planet?

How did you go? Turn to page 228 to find out and then RACE back because the party doesn't start till you return!

ONWARD AND UPWARD

☆ ☆

Everyone, look! It's the guest of honour themselves.

Happy Imagineering Academy graduation!

I declare MISSION SPARKOLOGY a BIG blinkin' success.

Here's your certificate.

CERTIFICATE

I, Captain Kilowatt, hereby award you

_____
codename

a certificate of imagineering from the

Imagineering Academy. This certificate certifies

that you are an enviro-superhero who excels

in the art of banishing phantoms that suck

energy, identifying fossil-fuel climate culprits and

imagineering solutions for a renewable future in

the blink of an eye.

Captain Kilowatt

Bravo! The crowd goes wild! CONGRATULATIONS!

Before you go, I've got some final words of wisdom for you. The truth is you can learn all the science and engineering on the planet and imagineer all day every day. But these lessons have taken many imagineers further than any academy training can.

1. Take care of yourself

Taking time to think and breathe is as important as remembering to eat your breakfast. Just as our daily lives use a lot of energy, so do our bodies and minds. You have to take care of yourself to be able to help save the whole blinkin' planet!

2. Work together

Success comes from teamwork and cooperation with people who have different skills and ideas. Imagineering is one important skill, but there are many other skills out there that your teammates and friends can contribute when you're working toward the same goal.

3. Don't leave anyone behind

People from all walks of life call our planet home and everyone needs to be included. Spread the word far and wide about the problems we face and try to make sure you're not leaving anyone out when you come up with solutions.

There are many ways to save the whole blinkin' planet whether you plant trees, compost food waste or imagineer new types of renewable energy. You can't do everything at once, but you also don't have to choose just one way to save the whole blinkin' planet.

For me, imagineering is everything. I hope your imagineering skills will come in handy, no matter where your next adventure takes you.

To bring this adventure to a close and start a new one beyond this book, repeat after me . . .

PLEDGE FOR THE BLINKIN' PLANET

I, Captain Kilowatt,

. . . no, you're not Captain Kilowatt! You say your own name!

I, [codename] _____ also known as

[real name] _____,

swear to keep blinkin' thinkin'

about problems big and small,

and to keep devising and designing

seriously super solutions.

I swear not to be afraid

to try new things and test my ideas.

But mostly I swear to share this adventure with others

because heroes don't work alone.

I will join other everyday heroes

and won't leave anyone behind.

And I'll always stop for lunch.

Because you've got to fuel yourself to help out others.

Onward and upward!

LET'S SAVE THE WHOLE BLINKIN' PLANET!

ANSWERS

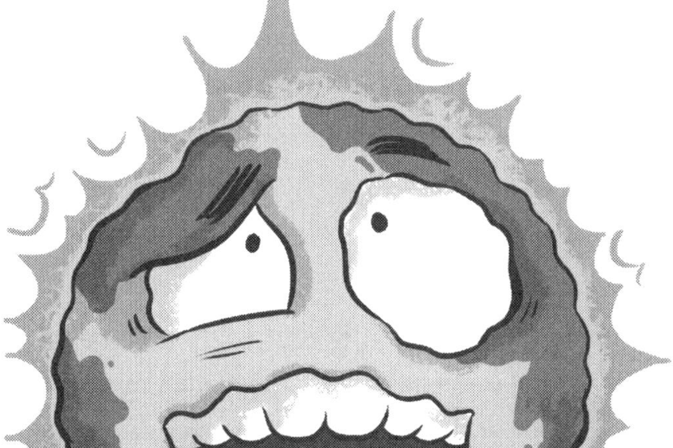

Those quizzical questions have illuminating answers. If you don't know the answer to any of the Lightning Quiz questions, then don't stay in the dark! Take a look at them here and come back any time to refresh your memory. Did you come up with a different answer? Could there be more than one answer to some of these?

You can write these answers down in your imagineering notebook. And if these questions and answers raise EVEN MORE questions, then write those down too. Following your curiosity is all part of the adventure!

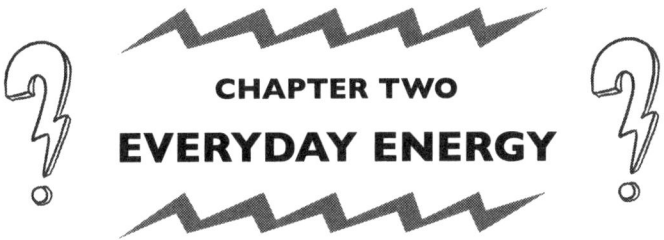

CHAPTER TWO
EVERYDAY ENERGY

1. What are the tiny, invisible, charged particles called that flow through electrical wires?

   Electrons!

2. What's one way you can keep the heat in your house during winter to save electricity on heating?

   Close the curtains, put something across gaps in doors or windows where a draft comes in, only heat the room/s you are using, use an energy-efficient heater like a wall-mounted reverse-cycle air-conditioner (if you have one).

   Hint: there are many more things that can be done. Think insulation and double-glazed or secondary-glazed windows, to name just a few. See the list of websites at the end of this book for more resources and ideas.

3. What should you do with electrical devices when you're not using them?

Switch them off at the wall.

4. What is the name of the energy sucker we just defeated?

Phantom Power!

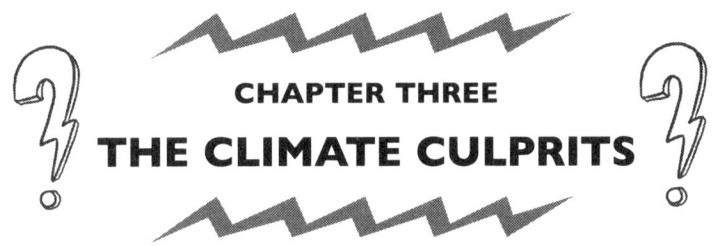

CHAPTER THREE
THE CLIMATE CULPRITS

1. What are the three types of fossil fuels that I like to call the climate culprits?

   Coal, oil and gas (AKA fossil gas, AKA methane, AKA natural gas).

2. Why are they called fossil fuels?

   They are made from plants and animals that died, were buried, and broke down and changed a long time ago when lots of fossils were formed.

3. How long did it take for fossil fuels to form? Months, years, hundreds of years, or hundreds of MILLIONS of years?

   It took hundreds of millions of years!

4. Why is using fossil fuels so blinkin' bad for the planet?

   Using fossil fuels causes greenhouse gases like carbon dioxide (CO_2) to be made and released into the atmosphere. Greenhouse gases cause the planet to warm, which changes our climate. And that has impacts on health, habitats, extreme weather and more!

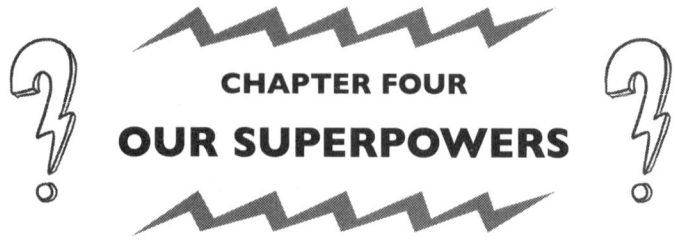

CHAPTER FOUR
OUR SUPERPOWERS

1. What does it mean if something is renewable?

    It means something can be replenished or replaced as quickly or faster than it is used.

2. Are fossil fuels – coal, oil and gas – renewable or non-renewable?

    Non-renewable.

3. What is one type of renewable power we can use to help the planet?

    Solar power, wind power or hydropower. Hint: there are other correct answers too!

4. Is it better to cooperate with each other as a team or try to tackle all the planet's problems at once as a lone ranger?

    It's better if we work together and cooperate as a team! We can achieve so much more that way.

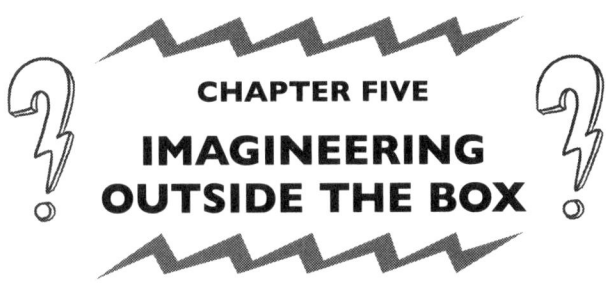

CHAPTER FIVE

IMAGINEERING OUTSIDE THE BOX

1. Where does the heat used in geothermal energy come from?

Way underneath the ground in the Earth's core!

2. Where does France get most of its energy?

Nuclear power.

3. What technology helps to store solar power when the Sun doesn't shine and wind power when the wind doesn't blow?

Batteries.

4. What do hydropower and pumped hydro storage have in common? Hint: it's the hydro . . .

Water movement is the key ingredient. Water is also called H_2O, which means hydrogen dioxide. That's where the 'hydro' part of these words comes from.

5. How's your sandwich? Are you going to eat the rest of that?

Just joking! It's all yours. You need your energy.

CHAPTER SIX

GRADUATION

1. What are the four stages of the innovation cycle?

   Think, Design, Make, Test.

2. What is a greenhouse gas?

   Greenhouse gases are invisible molecules in the air that float into the atmosphere when we burn fossil fuels. These include carbon dioxide (CO_2), methane and other gases that trap heat from the Sun in our atmosphere, causing the Earth's temperature to rise and changing the weather systems and the climate.

3. What are the tiny invisible everyday heroes that make electricity possible?

   Electrons!

4. What is the name of the eco-villain who saps energy from your electronics when you're not using them?

Phantom Power, otherwise known as Phantom Energy.

5. What does 'renewable' mean?

It means something can be replenished or replaced as quickly or faster than it's used.

6. Name the three fossil-fuel climate culprits that create greenhouse gases.

Coal, oil and gas (AKA fossil gas, AKA natural gas, AKA methane).

7. Name two sources of renewable power.

The Sun, water and wind are big ones, but there are a lot more. Geothermal and nuclear energy are just some of the others.

8. What important material is used to make solar panels?

Solar panels are made up of lots of small sections called solar cells. Solar cells are made with a really thin layer of a material called silicon.

9. Where can you store Sun and wind energy when the wind doesn't blow and the Sun doesn't shine?

Batteries!

10. What is one important use for batteries that can help save the blinkin' planet?

They can store energy so that electric vehicles can move without petrol or other fossil fuels.

GLOSSARY

Need to know more about a word you've seen?
Check out this list of wise words and their
meanings in this glossary (that's a word that
means a list of words and their meanings,
by the way).

ATMOSPHERE

The layers of air (a mix of different invisible gases) that wrap around our planet.

ATOMS

The tiny little invisible bits that make up everything! There are many different types of atoms that can connect with each other to make elements and molecules. Atoms are made from even SMALLER parts (including electrons).

BATTERIES

Devices that store electrical energy so that it can be used later.

CARBON DIOXIDE (CO_2)

Carbon dioxide is an invisible, odourless gas. It is a greenhouse gas molecule made from one carbon atom joined to two oxygen atoms. That's why people sometimes call it CO_2.

CIRCUIT

A connected route or pathway that starts and finishes in the same place. An electric circuit is a completely connected path that electricity flows through.

CLIMATE

The pattern of weather conditions in an area over a long period of time (at least thirty years).

CLIMATE CHANGE

The shift in temperature and weather patterns in an area over time. Since the 1800s, humans have caused the climate to change much faster and the planet to warm due to greenhouse gases in our atmosphere trapping heat from the Sun.

COAL

A type of black or brown rock that formed deep underground over millions and millions of years. It can be burned to create electricity, but this process also causes the creation of greenhouse gases like carbon dioxide.

DAM

A wall built across a river to hold water back and stop it from flowing. The wall can then be raised to allow water to flow in a controlled way to generate energy and make electricity.

ELECTRIC VEHICLES

A form of transport (e.g. a car or bus) with an engine that runs on electricity rather than petrol, diesel or any other form of fuel. These vehicles have a battery that can be charged by plugging into an electricity source.

ELECTRICAL CURRENT

The flow of electrons.

ELECTRICAL ENGINEER

Someone who designs, makes and fixes things that run on electricity. They are good at using science to solve problems!

ELECTRICITY

A form of energy that can be used to power electrical things. This energy comes from the flow of electrons.

ELECTRONS

Tiny particles that whiz around the outside of atoms. When these particles flow along a path this is called an electric current.

ENERGY

The capacity to do work that makes things move or change; the exertion of power.

EXTREME WEATHER

Unexpected or severe weather events. For example, blizzards, cyclones, floods, heatwaves, hurricanes and droughts.

FILAMENT

A thin thread-like wire in an old-fashioned incandescent light bulb that lights up when electricity flows through it. Most light globes are LEDs now, which are much more power efficient and work in a different way.

FISSION

When the centre of an atom splits in two.

FOSSIL GAS

Also sometimes called natural gas or just gas.

FOSSIL FUELS

Substances including coal, oil and fossil gas that formed from dead plants and animals over millions and millions of years underground. These substances can be burned to create energy, but they also produce greenhouse gases that cause climate change.

FUGITIVE EMISSIONS

Greenhouse gases that leak out or escape into the atmosphere, usually from fossil-fuel industries.

GENERATOR

A device that turns movement (or burning fuel) into electricity.

GEOTHERMAL ENERGY

Heat from the Earth's core that can be used to create electricity and other kinds of power.

GREENHOUSE GASES

Invisible molecules in the air that float into the atmosphere when we burn fossil fuels. These include carbon dioxide, methane and other gases that trap heat from the Sun in our atmosphere, causing the Earth's temperature to rise and changing the weather systems and the climate.

HYDROELECTRICITY

Electrical energy created using the movement of water.

IMAGINEER

An engineer who uses their imagination to come up with creative solutions to problems.

INNOVATION CYCLE

The step-by-step process that helps you to create solutions to problems, test them out, and improve on them.

METHANE

A type of greenhouse gas that is the main ingredient in fossil gas, which we use to cook with and to generate electricity.

NON-RENEWABLE ENERGY

Energy (e.g. electricity or fuel) generated from sources that cannot be replenished as quickly as they are used (e.g. energy that comes from burning coal, gas or oil).

NUCLEAR ENERGY

Electricity generated from splitting the centre of an atom.

OIL

A liquid fossil fuel extracted from beneath the surface of the Earth. Ingredients that come from oil are used to make petrol and diesel that fuel cars, planes and other transport. Ingredients from oil are also used to make plastic.

OVERSUPPLY

Way more of something than is needed.

PEOPLE POWER

What we can achieve with all our efforts combined as a team.

PHANTOM POWER

The electricity used by an electrical device or appliance when it is not in use. For example, the standby light on appliances. Also called Phantom Energy.

POLLUTION

Something that is harmful to the environment (e.g. greenhouse gases).

POWER

The rate at which energy is transferred. Also a particular form of energy, e.g. nuclear power, electrical power, that gives us the ability to move, change or do things.

POWER STATION

Also called a power plant. This is a place where electricity is made and flows into powerlines to our homes.

POWERLINES

The long wires that electricity flows along.

RENEWABLE ENERGY

Energy (e.g. electricity or fuel) generated from sources that can be replenished as quickly as they are used (e.g. solar or wind power).

SOLAR POWER

Electricity made using energy from the Sun.

TURBINE

A large fan-like structure with propellers that turn when they are pushed by the wind so that this movement can be used to make electricity.

WIND POWER

Electricity made using the movement of the wind.

FURTHER RESOURCES

There's always more that even the brightest spark can learn and do! Here are some great websites to help you in your next fact-finding mission.

Australia Institute – australiainstitute.org.au

Australian Museum Climate Solutions Centre – australian.museum/learn/climate-change/climate-solutions-centre

Australian Renewable Energy Agency – arena.gov.au

Australian Youth Climate Coalition – aycc.org.au

Beyond Zero Emissions – bze.org.au

Bureau of Meteorology – bom.gov.au/climate

The Climate Council – climatecouncil.org.au

Department of Climate Change, Energy, the Environment and Water – dcceew.gov.au

First Nations Clean Energy Network – firstnationscleanenergy.org.au

School Strike 4 Climate Australia – schoolstrike4climate.com

SEED Mob – seedmob.org.au

The Sunrise Project – sunriseproject.org

WWF Australia – wwf.org.au

Still got big questions about energy and climate in your local area?

Check your local council website or ask your local member of parliament for more information. Many local councils have great programs and resources supporting sustainability and renewable energy in practical ways.

Volunteering with a local environment, wildlife or conservation group is also a great step. There are lots of fellow planet savers out there doing powerful things and sharing their skills and knowledge!

ACKNOWLEDGEMENTS

I would like to thank Tim Baxter for lending me his sharp climate-focused mind and providing feedback and suggestions as an expert and a dad. Thanks also goes to Dr Matthew Priestley from UNSW Digital Grid Futures Institute and to Ketan Joshi, who both lent their expert eyes to the final draft. Thank you to all the scientists, engineers, policy experts and other researchers who work tirelessly to ensure that communicators like me and the wider public have access to the best possible information to tackle the world's big blinkin' problems. I would also like to thank my lovely IRL and online friends for providing me with constant support and enthusiasm along the way. And to Jason – you're the absolute best and I couldn't do it without your love and support!

ABOUT THE AUTHOR

Lee Constable is a science and sustainability presenter and edu-tainer. She is best known for hosting Network 10 kids' science TV show *Scope*. Her TV appearances also include *Studio 10*, *ABC News Breakfast* and *War on Waste* (Season Three). Lee is the author of *How to Save the Whole Stinkin' Planet: A Garbological Adventure*.

Growing up on her family's sheep farm in rural New South Wales during severe drought inspired Lee to pursue her interest in science, climate and the environment in a Bachelor of Arts/ Bachelor of Science (Honours). While studying a Masters of Science Communication she toured remote and regional Australia in the Questacon Science Circus, hosted a radio show on 2XXFM and SYN Nation, and founded Co-Lab: Science Meets Street Art. Lee's other adventures included guiding night-time spotlight tours of the National Botanic Gardens, giving tours of a landfill and recycling sorting facility and commentating robot battles.

In 2018, Lee embarked on an Antarctic journey as part of an all-women-in-STEM voyage. She used this experience to create *Antarctica: The Twitch-u-mentary* – an eight-hour livestreamed interactive edu-taining experience on her Twitch channel where she also talks science.

Lee regularly presents Instagram and Tiktok explainer videos for her own channels as well as other organisations and works as an MC and freelance science and sustainability communicator. In her spare time, she enjoys scuba diving and delivering science-y stand-up comedy routines as her Drag King alter ego Milton MANgo. You can find Lee constantly babbling on all social media platforms as @Constababble.

ABOUT THE ILLUSTRATOR

Aśka, (pronounced 'Ash-ka'), is creative dynamite! She's an energetic visual storyteller, an ex-quantum physicist and a talented science communicator.

A hugely engaging and popular presenter, Aśka is passionate about visual literacy. She has published more than ten books, comics and graphic novels; in Australia and overseas. Her recent titles include the YA graphic novel *Stars in Their Eyes* (with Jessica Walton), which was a CBCA Notable Book, and shortlisted for the ALIA Graphic Award and Comic Arts Award Australia. Recently the book was re-released by Graphix (Scholastic) for the American market, where it was awarded the prestigious Stonewall Honour Book award.

Aśka is also a recipient of several Australian arts grants, prizes and fellowships. When she's not creating books, Aśka helps organise comics festivals, runs live comics reading events and spends her time volunteering for her local communities of book creators and makers. She can also be found travelling across Australia, teaching drawing-as-a-language to enthusiastic audiences of all ages. Sometimes, she sleeps.

To find out more about Aśka and her latest projects you can follow her on Instagram at @askastorytelling, or go to her website: www.askastorytelling.com.

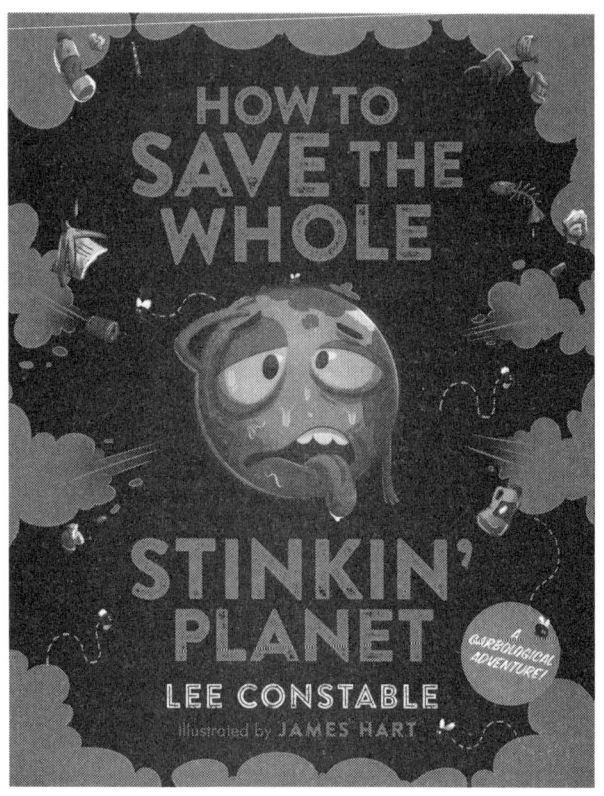

Let's go on a journey – it's going to be stinky, sticky and pretty gross, but if you want to be a waste warrior it's the most important journey you'll ever take.

HOW TO SAVE THE WHOLE STINKIN' PLANET
will take you on a garbological adventure like no other. From diving into the rubbish bin and delving into landfill, to rummaging through the recycling and digging about in compost.

As a waste warrior in training, you will earn badges as you work your way through each chapter, completing activities, DIYs and eco-experiments. Every part of this training will enhance your understanding of waste management and the impact our household rubbish is having on the (stinkin') planet.

A NOTE ABOUT THE BOOK

To ensure the carbon footprint was decreased for the production of this book, it was printed locally in Australia.

Our printer ensures all waste paper, cardboard, plastic and aluminium is 100% recycled. They have been working on reducing their company waste to landfill and all paper and board they purchase is 100% FSC certified.

The Forest Stewardship Council (FSC) is an international organisation that promotes responsible management of the world's forests. It does this by setting standards on forest products, along with certifying and labelling them as eco-friendly.

This book has a durable cover that is designed to last. Keep it, share it and pass it on. To recycle, just take off the front and back cover and put the book in a paper recycling bin.

Our publisher Penguin Random House Australia is committed
to focusing on how they can innovate and improve to reduce
the environmental impact of their operations. It is their goal
to ensure sustainability underpins everything they do and to
consider the role they play within society in combating the
climate emergency.

Penguin Random House Australia has a proud history of
publishing vital and wide-ranging content about climate change
and sustainable practices, as well as books that help people make
practical changes in everyday life.

www.penguin.com.au/sustainability